Baseball in the
MAHONING VALLEY

=== FROM PIONEERS TO THE SCRAPPERS ===

Baseball in the
MAHONING VALLEY

FROM PIONEERS TO THE SCRAPPERS

PM KOVACH

THE
History
PRESS

Published by The History Press
Charleston, SC
www.historypress.com

Front cover, top left: Mahoning Valley Scrappers; *top center*: author's collection; *top right*: Mahoning Valley Scrappers; *bottom*: Thomas Drake.
Back cover: Mahoning Valley Scrappers.

First published 2023

Manufactured in the United States

ISBN 9781467151986

Library of Congress Control Number: 2022949546
Notice: The information in this book is true and complete to the best of our knowledge. It is offered without guarantee on the part of the author or The History Press. The author and The History Press disclaim all liability in connection with the use of this book.

Dedicated to the late Paul F. Kovach, Salvatore Marino and "Smalley" Smolka. "The Longest Home Run in Baseball History" is dedicated to Robert Mertes.

CONTENTS

CONTENTS

ACKNOWLEDGEMENTS

Thanks to wife, Kathleen; son, Alex Kovach, his wife, Lisa; and my daughter, Gabrielle Lageson, and her husband, Dan.

Thanks to Tom Drake, John Brown, the Niles Historical Society (especially curator Audrey John). Ditto for Pamela Spiers from the Mahoning Valley Historical Society, the Cleveland Public Library, Cleveland University (especially Elizabeth Piotrowski) and the entire Mahoning Valley Scrappers organization (especially Matt Thompson).

Special thanks to Marty Tacsik and Chuck Nader.

KRAKATOA

For the heart of Indonesia, it was a "day without dawn." For twenty-one hours, plumes of sulfurous fogs and ash spewed forth from the volcano Perboewatan on the uninhabited Pacific island of Krakatoa, blotting out the sky with dark clouds of lethal gases and deadly shoots of fiery hot magma. The island, located in the Sunda Straight waterway between the Indonesian islands of Java and Sumatra, exhibited newly formed fissures and breeches in the granite crust, auguring for weeks the unholy unleashing of the "gates of hell." Finally, on Monday, August 27, 1883, at 10:02 a.m. local time, "Fire Mountain" erupted with the loudest paroxysm in modern history. The sixty-thousand-year-old island once known for its abundance of fragrant spices and exotic tropical fauna vaporized in the explosion with "billions and billions of tons of rubble and dirt disappearing forever" into the atmosphere. The reverberation was heard in the Indian Ocean three thousand miles away. Shockwaves circled the globe seven times, resulting in a 140-foot water wall that completely immersed the nearby islands of Poeloe Temposa, Sebuku and Sebesi. Minutes later, the tsunami annihilated the entire district of Tjiringin, killing 10,000 people and causing massive destruction to the port cities of Anjer, Telok Betong, Ketimbang and Batavia in southern Sumatra and western Java. In all, 165 coastal villages were utterly devastated. The final death toll from the tsunami reached 36,417. In the violence, scores of dead washed ashore as far away as Zanzibar in eastern Africa.

Krakatoa, contemporary drawing, circa 1883. After the eruption, famed English poet Gerard Manley Hopkins (1844–89) waxed eloquent about the changing heavens above: "The ground of the sky in the east was green or else tawny, and the crimson only in the clouds. A great sheet of heavy dark cloud, with a reefed or heavy make, drew off the west in the course of the pageant: the edge of this and the smaller pellets of cloud that filed across the bright field of the sundown caught a livid green." Public Domain Review. *Library of Congress*.

In the aftermath, the earth's temperature cooled by several degrees, wreaking havoc on the growing season and crop yields. For years, cubic miles of pumice and debris enriched crepuscular clouds half a world away with a kaleidoscope of crimson and purple hues, reportedly the basis for *The Scream* (1893), the iconic expressionist masterwork by Norwegian artist Edvard Munch. British artist William Ascroft, living near the Thames River, painted during this time no less than 533 watercolors over the "course of his fascination." The global phenomenon also served as the inspiration for Frederick Edwin Church and other members of the nineteenth-century American landscape artists who scrambled to their canvas at twilight to record the angry sunsets.

And in the tiny village of Painted Post, New York, population 701 in the 1880 census, 10,207 miles from the volcano's epicenter, the deluge of rainfall that followed the cataclysm washed out forever the incredibly successful run of the traveling Niles, Ohio Grays baseball team. The Niles city nine, led by their star player, African American pioneer pitcher and future Cooperstown Hall of Famer Bud Fowler, had "took to the rails" of the New York Pennsylvania and Ohio Railroad, renaming themselves the

NYPANOs. Riding the rails of glory on Fowler's magnificent right arm, the independent team had somehow culled together an extraordinary record of forty-four wins against just eight losses against opponents in both the major and minor leagues, with Fowler accounting for a minimum of forty-two pitching victories.

As rainfall continued, the extremely wet and soggy conditions rendered unplayable all the ball fields of Steuben County and the surrounding area. Their fortunes savaged by the weather despite their success on the field, the NYPANOs had become, in essence, a traveling team with nowhere to go. Their meager funds at an end, the team wired their general manager for fifty dollars to return home.

Despite the weak squib of an ending, the scope and magnitude of Bud Fowler's pitching achievements, splashed across the newspapers of three states, became impossible to ignore. And despite the virulent systematic racism that survived the Civil War, organized baseball took heed. Fowler signed with the Stillwater franchise in the Northwestern League for the 1884 season. In his wake, the future Hall of Famer birthed a stellar tradition for baseball in the Mahoning Valley.

1

"DUSTIN' THE COBWEBS"

Doubtless, there are better places to spend summer days, summer nights than in ballparks. Nevertheless, decades after a person has stopped collecting bubble gum cards, he can still discover himself collecting ballparks. And not just the stadiums, but their surrounding neighborhoods, their smells, their special seasons, and moods.
—Thomas Boswell, How Life Imitates the World Series

*I*n the beginning, there was baseball.

Baseball: A bit of heaven on earth, where summers never end and the crack of the bat and the roar of the crowd sound eternal.

Minor League Baseball in the Mahoning Valley began in 1883 with two separate and distinct teams: the independent Niles Ohio Grays ball club and Youngstown in the Class D Western Interstate Association (formerly the Ohio Valley Baseball Association). And although Youngstown's roster that year boasted five players who later reached the National League—hometown sensation Jimmy McAleer, pitcher-outfielder Pit Gilman, infielder Ed "Jumbo" Cartwright and catchers Sim Bullas and Charlie Ingram—it was the Grays who received all the ink from contemporary sportswriters because of the unparalleled success generated by their African American pioneer pitcher, Bud Fowler.

History books list the first documented evidence of Bud Fowler's baseball career as a three-game trial with Chelsea, Massachusetts, in 1878. Later that year, pitching for Lynn Live Oaks of the International Association, Fowler beat the world champion Boston Red Caps by a score of 2–1. However,

Fowler himself, in a letter written shortly before his death, confirmed that his professional play began years earlier, during the season of 1872. At that time, Fowler would have been playing at the age of fourteen with the Neshannocks semipro ball club in New Castle, Pennsylvania. Like Niles, New Castle was a mecca for racial tolerance in the post–Civil War nineteenth century. The first African American ballplayer to reach the majors, Moses Fleetwood Walker, later played with that city in 1882.

To add yet another tantalizing piece of first-person evidence to his 1872 professional debut, when Fowler first arrived in Niles for tryouts, he strangely told Grays general manager Elmer Wilson that he was William Thompson from Cooperstown, New York, better known in baseball circles as Bud Fowler. As Fowler's real name was John Jackson, the pseudonym of William Thompson remains a puzzle. The only possible explanation is that Fowler believed that someone in the city would remember him playing by that name eleven years earlier with the visiting Neshannocks ball club. Indeed, Fowler would be instantly recognizable even after a decade. As later reported by future major leaguer Delos Drake, the son of William Drake, Fowler's onetime Niles, Ohio teammate who later sponsored a mixed-race team in Findlay Ohio, Fowler as an African American had one very distinct physical characteristic, the result of a condition called heterochromia: one blue eye and one brown eye. As a boy, Delos spent much time watching Fowler and later verbally confirmed this physical anomaly. Sadly, in 1872, neither Niles nor New Castle published a newspaper. So, despite the pieces of undeniable and provocative evidence provided by the ballplayer himself, written proof of Fowler's actual debut within the Valley remains impossible to confirm. And despite their success in 1883, the Niles Grays ball club did not survive the late-summer bankruptcy of the entire town.

Meanwhile, the Youngstown Puddlers, under new management, joined the ranks of the Iron and Oil League in 1884, acquiring rookie extraordinaire second baseman Ed McKean. The Grafton, Ohio power hitter would later prove to be one of the finest players of nineteenth-century Major League Baseball. McKean would reunite with Youngstown's Jimmy McAleer to form the heart of the National League Cleveland Spiders club in the 1890s, a team also populated by three pitchers with ties to the Valley: Nig Cuppy and Hall of Famers Cy Young and Bobby Wallace. Not surprisingly, because of the performances of these players, the Spiders reached the National League Temple Cup championship series in two successive seasons, winning the cup in 1895. (In the postseason celebration after Cleveland's victory, the Temple Cup was filled to the brim with liquor and tossed around like a football.) The following, written in March 1998 by *Niles Times* newspaper columnist Grace Allison on the eve of the resurrection of Minor League Baseball in the Mahoning Valley, retells a glorious tale of how the sport was born in Niles.

Dustin' the Cobwebs
By Grace Allison
The hottest subject…in the sports world here today in Trumbull County is the construction of a baseball stadium. Niles baseball was alive and well as early as the 1870s, and it is apparent we will soon be hearing the umpire calling "batter up." In 1830, baseball was a form of recreation across America and in 1842 the first organized baseball was founded. By the 1850s, landowners were maintaining baseball parks which they rented to ballclubs. During the Civil War, soldiers regularly played baseball to pass the time and to relax. The first professional baseball team played in 1869. During the 1872–73 season, the Oakland Baseball Club of Niles played at a field located between Pearl Street and Robbins Avenue near Lafayette Street. The club's lineup included Henry Baldwin catcher; C.H. Mason pitcher; Matt Schaefer first base; E.A. Biery second base; Ed Mackey third base; Charles Baldwin shortstop; and J.W. Robbins, George Arker, Jim Carr, and Craig Phillips in the outfield. In those days, the pitcher had to hold his arms straight and pitch. It was difficult to control the ball and the batter never knew if the ball was going to roll around on the ground or go into orbit. These players did not wear gloves, or any protection and the catcher always stood far behind home plate and caught the ball on the first bounce. To get his bat turned, the player had to take it to Warren. The player would walk to Warren, have his bat turned and hustle back to Niles to play in that afternoon's game. Teams came from nearby communities to play the Oakland Baseball Club. Niles' first semiprofessional baseball team called the Niles Grays, developed in 1883 through the efforts of Ed [sic] Wilson and his buddies, all of whom were members of the local amateur team. The NYPANOs as the team was known got its name by combining the initials of the New York, Pennsylvania and Ohio railroad, the predecessor of the Erie railroad. In the course of organizing the Grays, a Black man named Bud Fowler arrived in Niles.…Wilson quickly secured him as a pitcher for the team. Fowler was an exceptional player and could cover any position. Arrangements were made to play on a field bounded by South Main Street, Salt Springs Road, Third and Ward Streets. The Niles Grays made a good showing locally and eventually hit the road playing

teams across Pennsylvania and New York. After the team had been on the road for some time, they were unable to book games with competitive teams. Their manager sent a telegram to Niles: "We're stranded here. No dates arranged. What shall we do?" "Send $50!" Wilson sent the money, and the team came home.

By 1897, Niles had a baseball team that was number one in the area. That year on a Sunday afternoon, the Cleveland Wheeler club played the Niles Grays at Avon Park, in Girard, Ohio. A large number of the area baseball fans stayed in the park all night on Saturday to be assured of a good seat. The Niles team members were George England, a one-armed pitcher, Billy Cobb Kalb second baseman, Joe Conley first baseman, Charlie Crowe pitcher, Mutz Williams catcher and Eddie Wagstaff and Hoppy Burnett in the outfield. The Cleveland Wheelers were the star attraction in Northeastern Ohio at the time and most of the players came from other leagues across the country. Their outfielder Sockalexis was the first full blooded Indian to play in the big leagues. If he stayed from the "white man's" fire water, he was an outstanding player. Charlie Crowe and his boys were in rare form that day and defeated the Cleveland Wheelers 7 to 2.

2

BUD FOWLER, NILES, OHIO, AND THE 1883 BLUES/GRAYS GAME

Once my grandfather took me on the train to Des Moines to see Bud Fowler play. The old man fixed me with that eye of his and said there was not a man on this round earth who could out run or out throw Bud Fowler. I was pretty excited.
—*Marilyn Robinson,* Gilead

Fowler used to play second base with the lower part of his legs encased in wooden guards. He knew that about every player on a steal had it in for him and would, if possible, throw the spikes in him. About half the pitchers tried to hit the [African Americans] when they are at bat.
—The Sporting News, *March 23, 1889*

Bud Fowler has played match games for trapper's furs. He has been rung in to help out a team for the championship of a mining camp and bags of gold dust. He has played for Cowboys and the Indians. He has cross roaded from one town to another all over the far West playing for what he could get and taking a hand to help out a team.
—Cincinnati Enquirer, *1895*

The robber barons of old left something tangible in their wake.
—*Jerry Sterner,* Other People's Money: A Play in Two Acts

*T*he afternoon was scripted for baseball. The date was August 10, 1883. An overflow crowd of one thousand fans began arriving early via horse-drawn carriages, dusty buckboards and on foot to watch the first-place National League Cleveland Blues baseball team cross bats with the fans' beloved Niles, Ohio Grays ball club in an exhibition contest. The Blues versus the Grays, an irony not lost on the many Mahoning Valley veterans of the Civil War. The excitement was palpable. Special excursion trains brought the sporting gentry from the neighboring cities of Warren, Youngstown and Newton Falls to the recently constructed wooden grandstand at the outskirts of the Niles downtown city limits. Niles jeweler J.C. Kern announced the presentation of a handsome medallion at the end of the season to the Grays player with the best overall record. (In November 1883, NYPANOs star Charles Butler won the coveted commemorative medallion.) Fourteen-year-old Harry C. Davis walked the two-mile distance barefoot from Mineral Ridge, Ohio. Years later, Davis constructed his family dwelling on the right field area of what would forever prove to be his "home grounds."

Pitching for the Grays was a twenty-five-year-old African American from Cooperstown, New York, named Bud Fowler, the first Black professional ballplayer. The unbridled racism that followed the Civil War led to the unspoken color line in baseball, which barred Fowler from the major leagues and relegated him to playing in the low minors or with independent clubs like the Grays. Fowler knew well the Mahoning Valley. His professional career had commenced in 1872, thirty-six miles to the east in New Castle, Pennsylvania. At age twenty, Fowler's legend reached mythic status in the afterglow of his 1878 pitching victory against Harry Wright's world champion Boston Red Caps while playing for the Lynn, Massachusetts Live Oaks club. He defeated ace Tommy Bond, who had won forty games that year. Fowler's arsenal included an overhand drop pitch later known as a spitball. As Fowler remembered in 1904, "It was a ball of most uncertain destination and slipped off two wet fingers toward the plate." Fowler knew the ball would drop but could never tell if it would be four inches or a foot. The spitter was later deemed so dangerous that it was banned from Major League Baseball.

Fowler's deliverance to Niles was the stuff of legend. In late spring, Grays general manager Elmer A. Wilson and traveling manager Ed A. Blory were warming up on the practice field within sight of the Niles Erie Street train depot when the prospective hurler approached in street clothes and asked for a tryout, introducing himself as William Thompson, known in baseball circles as Bud Fowler. Mixing fastballs with off-speed pitches, Fowler's demonstration was dazzling. He was a major-league-caliber talent—except for the color of his skin. Wilson and Blory signed the newcomer on the spot.

William Thompson, aka Bud Fowler, was born John W. Jackson on March 16, 1858. A barber by trade, Fowler could effectively play any position, the supreme "ballist." Fowler honed his craft on the Cooperstown Seminary Campus, where, reportedly, future Union general Abner Doubleday had etched the first diagram of a baseball diamond into the hallowed dust around 1839. Fowler instantly transformed the Grays from "cupcakes to corn crackers." The Niles nine overpowered all opposition on the western whistle stops of the New York, Pennsylvania and Ohio Railroad, including two of the strongest semipro units on the continent, shutting out the Cleveland-based Southern All-Stars 8–0 and the K.C.'s of Cleveland by a score of 3–0. In the aftermath of their success, armed with a heady sense of invincibility fueled by youthful exuberance, folly and chutzpah, the Grays challenged the Cleveland Blues and were granted an open date on the schedule for a $150 guarantee, the equivalent of $3,540 today.

The Cleveland visitors arrived midmorning at the Erie Street depot and were feted with the finest twenty-five-cent breakfast along with longtime city mayor William Davis at the Sanford House hotel. Always with an eye for talent, Blues manager Frank Bancroft received the "skinny" on Warren right-handed hurler Lem Hunter, then playing for Toledo in the Northwestern League. Later that year, Hunter became the first Mahoning Valley native to reach the major leagues, pitching well in a mop-up game with the Blues.

As game time approached, Bancroft enlisted the services of the town's "official" horse-drawn hack to conduct the team in grand style to the field, presumably acquired from the April sale at public auction of the baseball "field, fence, and grandstand" in what was Bud Fowler's early haunting ground in New Castle, Pennsylvania. The items included "over 10,000 feet of lumber, mostly pine and grandstand with thirty 2 X 12 planks, 16 feet long."

The Blues' ascendancy in the National League standings was the result of a superlative pitching staff, including team ace Jim McCormick, "One Arm" Daily and rookie southpaw sensation Will Sawyer. The Blues had sterling defense at every position. In his first year at the helm, Frank Bancroft assembled what many consider to be one of the greatest defensive lineups of the nineteenth century. He signed two new catchers, veteran Doc Bushong and rookie Cal Broughton, and had a completely retooled outfield, including Tom York, Pete Hotaling and "Bloody" Jake Evans, arguably the finest catching gardener in major league history. The new catching corps and outfield complemented Cleveland's already potent "Stone Wall Infield" of Hall-of-Fame-caliber shortstop Jack Glasscock, double-play partner Fred Dunlap at second base and Mike Muldoon (third base) and Bill Phillips (first base) on the corners. For this trip, bowing to the demands of a tight pennant race, Bancroft left behind McCormick, Daily, Sawyer and frontline catchers Bushong and "Fatty" Briody, utilizing instead a Harvard collegian pitcher named Edwards with Broughton behind the plate.

The game held special importance of pride for Niles residents, who endured "Black Friday" just two weeks before, on July 26, 1883, when the town's A.G. Bentley and Company Bank and two foundries, the Niles Iron Company and the L.B. Ward Company, declared bankruptcy, simultaneously shuttering their doors at 10:30 a.m. The factories had restructured and survived the nationwide economic turmoil of 1871–73, only to succumb to the price manipulations of robber baron Andrew Carnegie, who ruthlessly undercut all competitors as the cost for steel rails plummeted from seventy-one dollars a ton in 1880 to twenty dollars a ton. With the economic uncertainty, several residents simply scaled the fence and watched the game's proceedings from the outfield.

For Grays fans, the unfortunate recent curse of fate continued when Stonewall infielder Bill Phillips brought along his lucky souvenir alligator tooth and slammed a titanic bases-clearing home run in an eight-run second inning, opening the floodgates to a 25–3 rout of the hometown club. Slugger Charles Butler, Fowler's regular battery mate and the Grays' best hitter, was oddly absent for this all-important contest. None of the four substitute catchers could hold Fowler's fastballs in this gloveless era, leading to fourteen unearned runs. The defensive play of that game was a breathtaking, rally-killing out at first base by Cleveland's Pete Hotaling from the nether regions of center field. For the Grays, twenty-year-old medical student and left fielder William H. Drake hammered two of the team's eleven hits and scored a run. Drake also struck an intense friendship/partnership with teammate Bud Fowler that endured until death. Indeed, a decade later, the two men reunited to form the wildly successful Findlay, Ohio Sluggers independent ball club with another African American, Grant Johnson.

At the time of their visit, the Blues stood atop the standings in the National League pennant race with a little more than a month remaining. Three teams were within a game and a half of the lead: the Providence Grays, led by right-handed hurler Hoss Radbourn; Cap Anson's Chicago Colts; and the Boston Beaneaters. Unfortunately, Blues ace Jim McCormick suffered a season-ending arm injury shortly after that Niles game. But despite the loss of their best pitcher, the Blues soldiered on, losing then regaining first place for a single day in the wake of One Arm Daily's September no-hitter on a rain-sodden field in Philadelphia, before the Blues relinquished the lead for good. The pennant race among the four contenders continued to the wire. Overworked and unable to overcome late-season injuries to key players, the tattered Blues remained in the chase for the flag until the final three-game series of the season, when the soon-to-be-champion Boston Beaneaters swept Cleveland. The Blues had come up short in one of the closest pennant races in NL history.

Six days after the Blues/Grays contest, with vanishing gate receipts due to the closing of the factories, Fowler and company took to the rails as the featured attraction of a two-game series with Pittsburgh's East Liberty Stars to open their new stadium on Larimore Street. With a capacity of four hundred, the stadium was an anomaly, composed entirely of bleacher seating. Following the Pittsburgh series, and with little more than a wing and a prayer, the nine-man traveling team rechristened themselves the NYPANOs and began a month-long barnstorming tour. Coined from the initials of the New York, Pennsylvania and Ohio Railroad, the NYPANOs played teams from the Western Association, Carlisle University (Jim Thorpe's alma mater) and various railroad whistle stops in Pennsylvania and lower-state New York. In all, the athletes traveled 1,265 miles on the rails through seventeen cities. Their journey ended with a whimper with their funds depleted in the unlikely locale of Painted Post, New York.

Fowler played but did not pitch in the final contests. The cause was hinted at in a pair of articles in the *Lancaster Intelligencer*, which referenced the ragged physical condition of the NYPANOs without mentioning Fowler by name. Fowler's stellar work for Niles had attracted the attention of the Northwestern League's Stillwater, Minnesota baseball club, which offered contracts to both Fowler and Charles Butler. An arm injury during his single season at Stillwater cause Fowler to permanently transition to second base. To history, Fowler is perhaps best remembered for his work at the keystone position. In 1884, he batted .302 and led the Northwestern League in hits. The Stillwater team disbanded at season's end. Johnny Peters and Fowler were picked up by the Keokuk, Iowa ball club in 1885. After reuniting with former teammate William H. Drake to form the nucleus of the Findlay Sluggers for three seasons, the Cooperstown native later enjoyed his greatest success with the Adrian, Michigan African American Page Fence Giants in 1895–96. Fowler's odyssey of diamond trails lasted thirty-one seasons through at least seventeen states in the far West, the Midwest and Canada. Fowler had warm remembrances of his time in Niles and often visited his former general manager, Elmer Wilson. Wilson fondly recalled that their

Bud Fowler (1858–1913) pictured with Keokuk in 1885, just two years removed from his spectacular forty-two-win season with the Niles, Ohio Greys/NYPANOs. The majority of Fowler's wins were against teams in the Western Interstate League. Bud Fowler was inducted into the Mahoning Valley Scrappers Days Gone By permanent signage exhibit and the National Baseball Hall of Fame on the same day, July 25, 2022. *Cooperstown Hall of Fame.*

reunions were happily animated and typically ended with the arrangement of a small "loan" to the former Niles standout.

The Blues/Grays game in Niles and its aftermath ushered in a renaissance in that city. Within a generation, favorite son William McKinley was twice elected president of the United States, entrepreneur Harry M. Stevens popularized both the scorecard and the hot dog via his concessionaire empire in ballparks and racetracks across the nation and future Cleveland Indians first baseman and 1926 American League MVP George H. "Tioga" Burns was born. The city's Eastwood Field is now home to the Mahoning Valley Scrappers, which for two decades was the Cleveland Indians' Class A farm team. An on-field tribute to Fowler, planned in 2020, was scrubbed when the entire minor league season was canceled due to the COVID-19 lockdown.

Fowler's 1883 sojourn in Niles was the most important of his life, leading directly to his 1884 signing with Stillwater. His three-year stint alongside fellow African American Grant Johnson (1891, 1893–94) with the Findlay,

The Niles, Ohio Chamber of Commerce Map, circa 1882. The South Main Street ball grounds were located within the lower third of the map, flanked between Main Street, Salt Springs Road and Ward Street. *Niles Historical Society*.

Ohio Sluggers, operated by Niles teammate William H. Drake, led to the formation of the Page Fence Giants in 1895–96. Fowler by this time had set up a permanent residence in Findlay, and he and Drake continued their collaboration until the end of the century.

Left: William Davis served as mayor of Niles from 1876 to 1894. During his final term of office, the village incorporated as a city of the second class. *Niles Historical Society*.

Right: Banker Anson G. Bentley was born in Brookfield Township in 1824. He achieved success during the California Gold Rush of 1849, returning a wealthy man and later founded two banks. *Niles Historical Society*.

Wracked with infirmities collected on countless baseball diamonds, the aftereffects of deliberate headshots at the plate designed to maim or kill and innumerable intentional spikings; bedridden, twisted and utterly forgotten, Bud Fowler died penniless at his sister's home on February 26, 1913, and was buried in a nameless pauper's grave. He was fifty-four years old. Fowler once said, "My skin is against me." Fowler's lament as an outlier in the world of his choosing was a cry of pain, a verbal fist raised to the inscrutable prejudice and mindless discrimination of the era. Yet it is his innate class and panache, as well as his overriding love for the great sport of baseball that echo through the pages of history.[*]

Bud Fowler was selected for baseball's Hall of Fame in 2022, the only resident of Cooperstown to be enshrined.

---

[*] On July 25, 1987, Bud Fowler's memory was resurrected with a special graveside service at the Oakview Cemetery in Frankfort, New York. Representatives from the National Baseball Hall of Fame, the Frankfort city mayor and baseball Hall of Famer Monte Irvin were on hand.

3

BASEBALL, CRIME AND
THE IGNOMINIOUS EXIT OF
JAMES WARD JR.

For James Ward Jr. and his family, the dire situation had become untenable. Just two weeks after Black Friday—the July 26, 1883 bankruptcy and simultaneous closure of the Niles Iron Company, the L.B. Ward Sheet Metal Works and the city's A.G. Bentley Bank— the growing desperation of the town's suddenly destitute steelworkers and their families had turned criminal with the clearly retaliatory attempted murder of the Wards' young son, James III. He luckily escaped injury after being a fired at with a rifle during an overnight camping trip on August 10 with four friends in the woods and wild that abutted his grandmother's Brown Street home. The Ward family (who were in Pittsburgh when the incident occurred) was left with little option but to abandon their efforts to reconstitute the two shuttered factories and forever pull up stakes in their hometown. County law enforcement officer Marshall Smelz investigated the episode and was unable to establish the identity of the perpetrator. The unfortunate incident took place close to the Ward family home just hours after an exhibition game between the Niles Grays baseball team and the National League's Cleveland Blues.

The crime had a special and cruel import for the Ward family. Nineteen years earlier, on the evening of August 27, 1864, at about 9:00 p.m., two Niles residents with a grievance on the rental property they occupied— widow Lydia Stephenson and her paramour, Francis O. Robbins—sought the proprietor, wealthy industrialist James Ward Sr., on the outskirts of one of the mills that he owned in the city. Stephenson's husband had been killed months earlier during the Battle of Kelly's Bridge, Kentucky, on March 17, 1863. "That the interlopers intended mischief was evident by the fact that both were armed." Fueled by anger and alcohol, the agitated pair first intercepted James Ward Jr., then aged twenty-three, near the furnace pits of his father's ironworks. A high-decibel argument ensued and quickly escalated into violence when Stephenson savagely struck at the young Ward with the hatchet she carried, knocking him senseless. When the senior Ward (who was nearby) rushed to intervene, Stephenson struck again, wounding the elder man with a glancing blow. Before her victim could recover, Robbins impetuously fired his Colt .45 revolver at point-blank range, the muzzle held so close that Ward's face was "blackened and scorched with gunpowder." James Ward Sr. was fifty years old when he was killed. The murderer, thirty, was described as an ex-soldier who was employed as a farmer. He was known as a thoroughly "dissipated and reckless man, a hard drinker who was frequently embroiled in fights" and was the prodigal son of Josiah Robbins, one of the wealthiest and most prominent citizens of Niles. Ward had built his "Russia Field" industrial complex on land once owned by Josiah Robbins.

Despite a $3,000 bounty for their capture ($48,407.50 in today's dollars), the brazen criminals managed to escape the city one step ahead of Marshal Butler and law enforcement. The pair commandeered a horse and buggy to Orangeville, Ohio, where they boarded the 4:00 a.m. Atlantic and Great Western Railway to Erie, Pennsylvania. The two then separated, taking different routes and transports to a planned rendezvous at Guleph, Ontario. It was there that the reunited couple was apprehended days later without incident by Cleveland deputy sheriff Michael Gallagher, accompanied by the Canadian Mounted Police.

The Francis O. Robbins trial commenced on December 1, 1864, in Warren's Trumbull County Court of Common Pleas with the honorable Judge Glidden presiding. The trial concluded four days later with Robbin's guilty verdict for second-degree murder. Stephenson had earlier pled guilty and received a ten-year sentence for second-degree manslaughter. Robbins was subsequently sentenced to life imprisonment.

Born on November 25, 1813, near Dudley, Staffordshire, England, James Ward Sr. emigrated to the United States with his family in 1817. Ward's father was an ironworker, and the "younger man obtained a knowledge of the business through his association with him." In 1842, "Messrs. James and brother William Ward and Mr. Russell under the name James Ward and Company erected a small rolling mill in Niles. They were all practical

Right: Industrialist James Ward Sr. (1813–1864) utilized European steel-making techniques and "black band" ore to produce a superior type of ferrous material. Ward's unrivaled success would later put the Niles mills directly into the crosshairs of his Pittsburgh rival, billionaire robber baron Andrew Carnegie. *Niles Historical Society*.

Below: In the wake of his father's untimely murder, industrialist James Ward Jr. joined with banker Anson G. Bentley to successfully restructure the Ward facilities through the Great Panic of 1873. By 1880, the Niles mills had become so successful that Ward was forced to expand his operations into New Philadelphia, Pennsylvania. *Author's collection*.

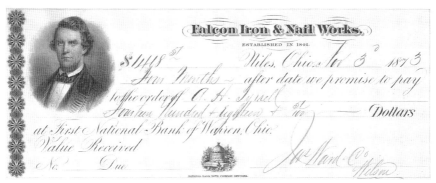

men…and for the first year performed most of the operations themselves. As time passed…they gradually enlarged their operations, until their business in all their ramifications employed five hundred men." At its peak, the rolling mill at the sheet-iron works was "330 feet in length and 100 inches in width with 14 boiling furnaces, 7 reheating furnaces [powered by two steam engines each 26 feet in length]….Three thousand tons of iron ore were manufactured yearly."

"Messrs. Ward and company also mine their own coal…at Weathersfield….The celebrated Black Band iron ore [thought formerly to be shale] underlines the coal, and the same bank thus furnished coal and ore. The indomitable perseverance and industry of…Ward and Company richly deserve the success they have achieved." The Ward family's brilliance in utilizing European ironmaking techniques and Black Band ore put the Niles manufacturing plants directly in the crosshairs of rival billionaire Andrew Carnegie, the Pittsburgh industrialist who, in 1883, undercut all competitors, selling at a twenty-dollar-per-ton cost for iron.

Prior to the closure, the Ward Company employees were well paid, enabling a group of young sports-minded residents to form a professional club and construct ball grounds on South Main Street between Third and Salt Springs Road, complete with wooden fencing and a roofed grandstand. They assembled, player by player, one of the finest ball clubs of the era. An invitation to join the Iron and Oil League in November 1883 was declined. Days earlier, the Grays had officially disbanded due to lack of funds.

PRELUDE II

According to legend, Bud Fowler left his boyhood home in 1870, an African American explorer on the diamond trails. His extended stay in the Mahoning Valley marked the first time he played an entire season at one locale. In the process, Fowler formed personal bonds with several Valley citizens that endured until death. These fond and egalitarian relationships were unsurprising, given the Valley's sincere belief in the equality of all under God, regardless of skin color, a template distinctly at odds with the virulent racism of the nineteenth century. And when the Civil War arrived on its doorstep, the Mahoning Valley responded unwaveringly with its service and blood to abolish the abhorrent practice of slavery. The citizens' mettle was severely put to the test at the Battle of Franklin, Tennessee.

4

OPDYKE'S MAHONING VALLEY TIGERS AND THE BATTLE OF FRANKLIN, TENNESSEE

One hour ago, this fair street was a thing of beauty. I can not walk upon the sidewalks now. They are covered with wounded, dying, and dead Men.
—Keesy, Sixty-Fourth Ohio Volunteer Infantry

The late autumn sky was a deep burnished orange on the afternoon of November 30, 1864. Soon, the parched earth would be awash in blood as twenty-five Confederate regiments under the command of General John B. Hood surged forward against the entrenched Union forces just outside the town of Franklin, Tennessee. It was the twilight of the War between the States, and Hood's Army of Tennessee was increasingly the last vestige of hope for victory in the South. Earlier that day, Hood had eschewed the recommendation of his ablest commander, Nathan Bedford Forrest, to utilize the cavalry to attack the enemy flanks. Hood opted instead for a full-frontal assault against the Union army. The rebel general hoped his numerical superiority would carry the day. He seriously underestimated the tenacity of Union colonel Emerson Opdyke and the Tigers of his command, the 125th Ohio Volunteer Infantry (OVI). The Ohioans' incredible courage under fire proved to be the decisive factor in the battle. Opdyke had faced Hood once before, in September 1863 near Chickamauga Creek. In that battle, Hood lost his leg in the victory; he had to be strapped into the saddle for the duration of the war. Opdyke and his Tigers, meanwhile, saw action at Atlanta; Chattanooga; Resaca, Georgia, where the colonel was severely wounded; Lost Mountain; and Shiloh,

Tennessee. Opdyke is best remembered by contemporary historians for his actions that day at the Battle of Franklin.

Born in Hubbard, Ohio, in 1830, Samuel Emerson Opdyke became a leather merchant and was an ardent abolitionist who detested slavery and all those who supported its cause. When war came, Opdyke partnered with Seth Bushnell of Hartford, Ohio, to form the 45th Ohio Volunteer Infantry in the earliest days of the conflict. Commissioned first lieutenant in 1861, Opdyke proved fearless under fire and, despite his lack of military training, rose to the rank of captain the following year. The leather merchant felt strongly that it was his solemn duty to facilitate and redirect the souls of newly departed rebels into the fires of hell. Wounded on the field of battle, Opdyke later resigned his commission. During his convalescence, he returned to Ohio to form the 125th Ohio Volunteer Infantry, largely from the citizenry of the Mahoning Valley. Nicknamed the Tigers for their cool bravery under fire, the unit would face its sternest challenge at Franklin. Before the battle, Colonel Opdyke had differed with one of his commanding officers, Brigadier General George Wagner, about the placement of his Tigers. The exchange grew heated. Finally, the general is reported to have said, "Well Opdyke, fight where and when you damn please, we all know you'll fight."

Fight they did.

The battle began about four o'clock in the afternoon, when twenty-two thousand Confederate foot soldiers charged ahead four hundred yards marching to the strains of "Bonnie Blue Flag" and "Dixie." It was one of the few times that the gray-shirted "tooters fought alongside the shooters." As the Confederates approached, Union sharpshooters took deadly aim at the enemy. Yankee cannons fired volley after volley of "grape and canister," releasing deadly waves of shrapnel into the Southern ranks.

Despite heavy casualties, the rebels pressed forward, finally breaking through the Union defenses at two places, a farmhouse owned by Fountain Branch Carter and at the site of Carter's cotton gin. Seizing the opportunity, Confederate general Patrick Cleburne rallied his men into the gap. At that moment, Opdyke ordered his men to cut off their backpacks for mobility, and the vastly outnumbered Tigers met the enemy head-on in fierce and deadly hand-to-hand combat. With the use of bayonets and rifle butts, the hellish fighting continued at close range. Acrid smoke from the surrounding musket and cannon fire were so thick that it was impossible to see more than a few feet. Five Confederate generals died trying to advance; a sixth was carried from the field mortally wounded. Many historians consider the encounter to be the most intense fighting in the entire Civil War. Finally, the Southerners were beaten back to an outer ditch surrounding the Carter farm. It quickly became a killing field. Unable to advance or retreat, hundreds of rebels were slaughtered in their tracks. After five hours, the Army of Tennessee was routed from the field of battle, a decisive Union victory.

General George Thomas thankfully praised the 125th OVI after the conflict. Opdyke was subsequently promoted to the rank of brigadier commander. After the war, he settled in New York and ran a dry-goods store. In 1884, Opdyke fatally shot himself in the stomach while cleaning his pistol. He was fifty-four years old. Opdyke is interred at Oakwood Cemetery in Warren, Ohio. On July 4, 1890, a stone memorial honoring those Valley veterans who served was dedicated in the western quadrant out of the Warren, Ohio Trumbull County Courthouse square.

In 2000, a dozen reenactors of the 125th Ohio Volunteer Infantry traveled fourteen hours from their home base on Stone Mountain, Georgia, to pay their respects to the memory of Opdyke in a solemn graveside ceremony in Warren. The group placed a wreath on the general's grave and fired three volleys from their muskets into the air, a fitting tribute to the courage of Opdyke and all those who served from the Mahoning Valley.

There are several interesting facts about the Battle of Franklin. More generals were killed in the battle than in any other battle in modern warfare. In 1865, after his hellish loss at Franklin and a later defeat at Nashville, John Bell Hood resigned his commission in disgrace. After the war, he settled his family in New Orleans and later died in the yellow fever epidemic of 1870.

At Franklin, Irish-born Confederate general Patrick Cleburne had two horses shot out from under him and died in a hail of gunfire while leading his men forward. His wife learned of his death from a paper carrier shouting the news from the nearby street.

One of the Southerners killed in battle was Captain Todd Carter, the twenty-four-year-

Union general Emerson Opdyke (1830–1884) formed the 125th OVI into his own image. The "Tigers" shock troops became known for their cool ferocity under fire and succeeded to turn the tide in hellish hand-to-hand combat against numerically superior opposition during the Battle of Franklin, Tennessee. Historians still debate whether Opdyke's death by self-inflicted gunshot was accidental or intentional. *Library of Congress.*

old son of Fountain Branch Carter, who was shot nine times trying to reach his boyhood home and died on the family kitchen table.

Nathan Bedford Forrest was named the Confederacy's chief cavalry officer in February 1865. After the war, he was involved with building railroads. He became fabulously wealthy after winning a lottery. He was also an active member of the early Ku Klux Klan, serving at its grand wizard from 1867 to 1869. He later resigned. The attacks from that group had grown too violent, even for him.

Fictional character Rhett Butler from Margaret Mitchell's epic novel *Gone with the Wind* was one of the "heroes" of the Battle of Franklin. The book recounts that Butler had been cited for bravery for his intense actions during the conflict by Confederate president Jefferson Davis.

According to historian Anne Colucci, the original regimental flag for the 125th currently resides at the Ohio Statehouse in Columbus.

The last known veteran's reunion for the Mahoning Valley survivors of the 125th OVI was held on November 17, 1913, at the GAR room in Warren, Ohio.

The Georgia reenactor group that celebrates the 125th OVI became enamored of the unit's history and permanently adopted the Tigers from Ohio, a rarity among such groups below the Mason Dixon line.

5

JIMMY McALEER, JUMBO CARTWRIGHT, ED McKEAN, THE RISE OF YOUNGSTOWN BASEBALL AND THE "CLEVELAND CONNECTION"

Jimmy McAleer was the best center fielder who ever was.
—Henry P. Edwards, Cleveland Plain Dealer

No one but McAleer could have made it.
—Harry Wright

The season is young yet.
—Joe Ardner, Chicago Tribune

They were "Brownlee's Beauties," Youngstown Ohio's 1884 entry in the minor circuit Iron and Oil League, featuring native-born outfielder Jimmy McAleer. Managed by T.P. Brownlee, it was indeed a beautiful baseball team. It also featured ambidextrous pitcher Owen Keenan, who beat the New Castle Neshannocks in both games of a July Fourth doubleheader that year, winning the morning game in New Castle, Pennsylvania, as a right-hander and, after boarding an excursion train to Youngstown, winning the afternoon game from the port side. Also on the roster were pitching ace right-hander William O'Donnell, change pitcher Jack Darrah, future Cleveland Spiders great and rookie sensation Ed McKean at second base and portly sophomore Ed "Jumbo" Cartwright at third. McAleer's outfield partners, Pit Gilman and Joe Ardner, played with the Cleveland Blue Stockings National League ballclub. Ardner later played against his former teammates. He would again reach the majors in 1890, playing with the Cleveland Spiders. Pitcher-outfielder Bones Ely also made the Youngstown roster that year and was elevated to Buffalo in the big show before season's end. Ely was tall for the time, measuring six feet, one inch and weighing a scant 155 pounds. Ely would remain in the majors well into the modern era.

The entire 1884 season proved remarkable. There were three major leagues: the American Association, starting its third season; the National League, dating from 1876; and the fledgling Union Association, which proved a one-year wonder. Big-league teams were in a record thirty-four cities. On May 1, 1884, African American catcher Moses Fleetwood Walker broke baseball's nineteenth-century MLB color barrier, taking the field for the Toledo Blue Stockings in the American Association. Chicago Cubs star Ned Williamson hit twenty-seven home runs to establish the single-season standard until Babe Ruth blasted fifty-nine in 1921 for the New York Yankees. Providence Grays pitcher Hoss Radbourn set the all-time win record with sixty-two victories, fifty-nine in the regular season and three more in the World Series, when the Grays swept the American Association champion New York Mets at the Polo Grounds. Former Cleveland Blues pitcher One Arm Daily notched a then record 483 strikeouts with two separate teams in the Union Association. And future Cleveland Indians player-manager Deacon McGuire became the first native Youngstowner to reach the major leagues, playing for the Toledo Blue Stockings in the American Association.

In 1884, with Bud Fowler toiling in the Northwestern League, Valley "sportswriters" began to appreciate the heretofore underrated Youngstown ball club. Speedster James Robert McAleer, born in Youngstown during the Civil War on July 10, 1864, proved to be a rare talent, elevating defense to an art form. Onetime Valley resident and future Hall of Famer Billy Evans reckoned that "McAleer was the first outfielder to take his eyes off the ball and [run to] the spot where it would land." Even as a teen, the affable Irishman was affectionately called the "Mayor of Youngstown." His genial nature served him well. Coupled with his diamond savvy, McAleer's baseball career spanned four decades as player, administrator, manager and finally owner of the Boston Red Sox. A mediocre hitter in the big leagues, McAleer sported a lifetime .255 batting average. It is agreed that whatever his deficiencies with the ash, McAleer's proficiency in the field atoned for that weakness.

McAleer's teammate, infielder Ed McKean, would have been weeks away from his fifteenth birthday when he made his debut on the Youngstown roster. Born on June 20, 1869, in Grafton, Ohio, McKean was a strapping lad who could wallop a baseball a country mile. Even as a youth, he had the arms of a stevedore, enabling him to lie and "add" five years to his actual age when he reported to Youngstown. McKean rose quickly thorough the minor league ranks and was the premier player on the Cleveland Blues when the franchise joined the ranks of the American Association in 1888. Youngstown native Deacon McGuire was also on the roster.

Born on October 6, 1859, in Johnstown, Pennsylvania, Edward Charles "Jumbo" Cartwright commenced his professional baseball career in 1883 with Youngstown. Cartwright had a breakout season with New Orleans in the Southern League in 1887, batting .430 and scoring thirty runs in his first sixteen games. Finally, in the latter part of the 1890 season, at the age of thirty, Cartwright signed with the St. Louis Browns, managed by Gus Schmelz in the American Association. Cartwright was thirty years old when he made his major league debut. "Jumbo" had an excellent half season, batting an even .300 with sixty RBIs in just seventy-five games. St. Louis finished a surprising third that year. Despite his performance, Cartwright was not retained for the following season and returned to the minors. In 1894, Schmelz became manager of the last-place Washington Nationals. He remembered Cartwright and installed the former Youngstowner at first base. Cartwright thanked his skipper by batting .294 and recording 106 RBIs in his first full season, at the age of thirty-four.

But in 1884, Cartwright and company were in their prime, ready to take on the world—or at least the Cleveland Blue Stockings, in an exhibition contest to promote their new downtown ballpark.

Meanwhile, the 1884 edition of the Cleveland Blue Stockings had changed from the successful squad of the previous season. It was a fractious ball club, riddled with dissention and discontent. Gone were manager Frank Bancroft, who would lead the Providence Grays that year to the World Series championship; 1883 team captain Tom York; second baseman Fred Dunlap; and fireball pitcher One Arm Daily. Not surprisingly given the losses in personnel, the Blues' fortunes quickly deteriorated as the team fell to the bottom of the standings. Subsequently, fan attendance fell to a whimper. Meanwhile, the Youngstowners' comparative success swelled the ranks of their fans to the point that the team had outgrown its digs at Bradley Park and necessitated the construction of a new home park on West Federal Street—the appropriately named West Side Park. An exhibition contest with the Blues to open the new ballpark was originally slated for July 3, 1884. When Cleveland opted out at the last minute, Youngstown manager T.P. Brownlee threatened to sue. The contest was hurriedly rescheduled for July 10.

On game day, the Clevelanders blew into town shortly before the afternoon start. "A large audience" was on hand. Pitching for the home team was ace William O'Donnell, with Joseph Sommers catching. For the Blues was right-hander Sam Moffet, with newly graduated dentist Doc Bushong behind the plate. Charlie Powers was the umpire. Three Blue Stockings players made a return trip to the Valley: former Youngstowner Joe Ardner in the outfield, Bill Phillips on first and Jack Glasscock at short. The batting order for Youngstown was as follows: Ed Cartwright, followed by first baseman Quinn, Jimmy McAleer, Pit Gilman in the cleanup spot, Miller at short, Ed McKean at second base, Baldwin in right, then O'Donnell and Sommers at the bottom of the order. Cleveland settled matters early, scoring six runs in the first frame. The finest hit of the game for either side was Ed Cartwright's "elegant" two-baser. The final: Cleveland 11, Youngstown 5.

Though the Youngstowners lost the exhibition game, the franchise scored an important victory with the city's horse-drawn trolley service, which agreed to provide transportation to and from the heart of the downtown business district to the outlying ball grounds, thereby insuring an encore season in 1885.

The Blues' fortunes crashed shortly after their Youngstown excursion. In August, amid rumors that the team was about to fold, three prominent starters, ace hurler Jim McCormick, infielder Jack Glasscock and catcher Fatty Briody, jumped to Cincinnati in the Union Association for a reported $1,000 each. Their surprise departure led to an opportunity for Youngstown's Pit Gilman, who was one of the talents signed in the Blues' desperate scramble to find replacement players of major league quality. In the end, the Cleveland franchise did not survive the perfidy of the "treacherous trio" and disbanded at the close of the season. Gilman's late-season departure also had a negative impact on Youngstown. The team's listless performance in his absence led to a tepid middle-of-the-pack finish in the Iron and Oil League standings.

During the long off-season, Youngstown manager T.P. Brownlee sustained serious injuries in a September harness race mishap at the Mahoning County Fair in nearby Canfield, Ohio. Brownlee eventually resumed his management duties for Youngstown's 1885 entry in the Interstate League. McAleer, McKean, Cartwright and Pit Gilman also returned. A total of eight starters reached the majors that year but the team finished third. The franchise ended its affiliation with Minor League Baseball but remained a viable independent team for several years. The Youngstown/Cleveland

Left: Jimmy McAleer (1864–1931), the first modern outfielder, models his Cleveland Spiders uniform. McAleer also had Olympic-caliber speed and once raced Pittsburgh professional sprinter Ed Nikirk. The winner of that race is still disputed. McAleer was inducted into the permanent signage of the *Mahoning Valley Scrappers Days Gone By* exhibit on July 25, 2022. *Author's collection.*

Below: The 1895 Washington Nationals with Youngstown player Ed Cartwright (1859–1933) (*second row, third from right*) and James Deacon McGuire (1863–1936) (*top row, far right*). *Author's collection.*

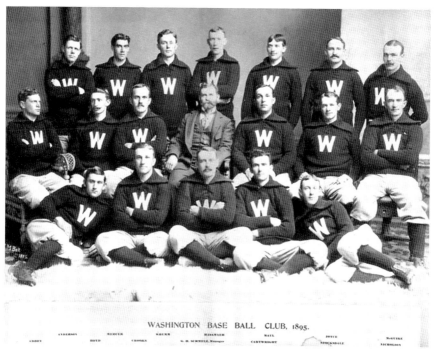

WASHINGTON BASE BALL CLUB, 1895.

Blues contest laid bare the fact that Jimmy McAleer, Ed Cartwright and Ed McKean were destined for better things, on the fast track to the big leagues.

Minor League Baseball returned to Youngstown in 1896, the team playing first as the Puddlers and later as the "Little" Giants, both entries in the Interstate League. Their resurrection would later play a prominent role in one of the closest, most exciting pennant races in Cleveland MLB history.*

---

* At the conclusion of his baseball career, Youngstown pitcher Owen Keenan became a professional musician with the Pittsburgh Orchestra. In 1908, Keenan became one of a select few persons in history to read his own newspaper obituary when it was mistakenly reported that he had died. Another prominent celebrity who read his own obituary: Nobel Prize–winning author Ernest Hemingway.

6

THE BALLAD OF BUD FOWLER, PARTS ONE AND TWO

Mahoning Valley Edition

The long War was done n' Abe Lincoln was dead.
Slavery was over and 'mancipation in its stead
Jim Crow was in vogue n' the "color line" drawn.
T'was an African American ballplayer n' this is his song
"Bud Fowler's the name and baseball's the game.
My skin is against me."
For thirty-one years he traveled around.
Playin' for gold dust in small minin' towns.
Cross-roading across the mid- and far West.
Playin' for trappers' furs, whatever he could get.
"Bud Fowler's the name and baseball's the game.
My skin is against me."
Growin' up in Cooperstown, learnin' the game.
Seminary Field will never be the same.
Playin' for pay at the age of fourteen,
with the New Castle Neshannocks, livin' the dream.
"Bud Fowler's the name and baseball's the game.
My skin is against me."
Whatever a team needed, Fowler's the cure.
Playin' for Niles, O., on their 1,000-mile tour.
"Bud Fowler's the name and baseball's the game.

My skin is against me."
Dying alone at age fifty-four,
Twisted painful n' bent, unable to give more.
Bury'd forever in a nameless pauper grave
The sins against him, he graciously forgave.
"Bud Fowler's the name and baseball's the game.
My skin is against me."
"So, here's to you Bud, our glass raised in toast,
Your great baseball career, proudly we boast."
"Bud Fowler's the name and baseball's the game.
My skin is against me."

BUD FOWLER AND WILLIAM DRAKE

The Greatest Story Never Told

By P.M. Kovach and Tom Drake

They cannot get a man equal to [Bud] *Fowler.*
—St. Louis Post Democrat, *May 9, 1884*

We shall always welcome any club that may be under Mr. Drake's management.
—Adrian Times and Expositor, *August 31, 1894*

Lethe: A river in Hades whose waters cause the souls of the dead to forget their life on earth.
—*Wikipedia*

In September 1891, life was altogether good for Bud Fowler. Having taken up residence in Watertown, Wisconsin (population 8,755), the pioneer African American second baseman had just completed a successful baseball season with a team sponsored by the town's clothing megastore Schiffler and Quentenmeyer. The independent club was known in the newspapers as the "S&Q's." Fowler's one-act musical play, *Colored Southern Aristocracy*, had piqued the curiosity and professional interest of the famed African American entertainers the Hyer Sisters and was possibly touring with a special theater troupe in midsized venues across Michigan and in the Carolinas under the name Colored Aristocracy. And his downtown barbershop, located at the Lee stand, was doing a brisk business. Indeed, in August, Fowler's tonsillar partner had pulled up stakes in the enterprise formerly known as Storm and Fowler and relocated his chair to Columbus, Wisconsin, some thirty miles distant.*

The weekly headlines Fowler provided throughout the summer with his sensational, heads-up play for the S&Q's doubtless helped fuel the decision to open a permanent field office for the *St. Paul Globe Democrat* in Watertown, located downtown on 110 Main Street in the Excelsior block sector. And by all available evidence, Fowler was much beloved by his newly adopted hometown, which had cheered his sterling defensive play and clutch hitting at the ballpark. And this presumably had forged his path to full citizenship and requisite acceptance in this staid, sleepy midwestern town. Some eight years after his triumphant 1,265-mile barnstorming tour with Niles across Ohio, Pennsylvania and New York State, and after playing two years in the Northwestern League, with countless destinations in between, Fowler had perhaps found a refuge, a place that could be a permanent home in the long years after baseball.

Yet it was not to be. Shortly after it was reported that Fowler had become Watertown's newest citizen, the ballplayer drank deeply from the waters of the Lethe River and left Wisconsin forever to reunite with his NYPANOs teammate, outfielder and doctor William Drake. In the years following his baseball excursion, Drake, who was born in Girard, Ohio, had established a thriving dental practice in Findlay, Ohio, and was looking to form a mixed-race team in his new hometown. Drake's 1888 arrival in Findlay to set up his soon-to-be lucrative professional practice coincided providentially with the emergence of African American slugger and shortstop Grant Johnson, a Findlay native then playing with the city's Leons club. Johnson would soon become the greatest ballplayer of the nineteenth century of either race; the first to hit sixty home runs in a single season. With Grant Johnson as the centerpiece and Bud Fowler spending increased amounts of time in Findlay, Drake had culled together a group of talented players from across the continent to fill the Findlay roster, including catcher Bobby Woods from Youngstown; pitcher Bill Reidy of Cleveland; Fred B. Cooke from Paulding, Ohio; and Howard Pastorius from Pittsburgh, Pennsylvania. They formed the nucleus of the semipro independent Findlay club that could rival all opposition, even

---

* There exists an obscure piece of nearly forgotten folk music called "Colored Aristocracy." The appearance of the tune seems to roughly coincide with Fowler's one-act musical of the same name, which would have been written during the off-season of 1890. Could Fowler have written the tune? The possibility is as intriguing as it is unknown.

MLB teams. Bud Fowler's baseball savvy and versatility was the missing piece to the roster.

In 1893, borrowing a page out of the NYPANOs playbook, the fledgling Findlay squad was scheduled to open their season with an exhibition against the Cleveland Spiders, but the game was washed out. Later that year, Findlay defeated the major league Cincinnati Reds by a score of 3–2, with Grant Johnson blasting two home runs off future Hall of Fame candidate Tony Mullane. The Findlays also beat the former MLB Detroit Wolverines with an 8–7 victory. Bud Fowler (not on the roster for the team photo), who rarely stayed in one place, broke his usual practice and remained long enough to play most of the season with Drake's ball club. Meanwhile, Grant Johnson put together one of the finest seasons in baseball history, blasting sixty home runs during this "deadest" period of the "Dead Ball" era and at once earning the sobriquet "Home Run" Johnson for himself and the subsequent renaming of the Findlay team to the Sluggers. (Grant "Home Run" Johnson is currently under consideration for induction into the National Baseball Hall of Fame in Cooperstown. The announcement is scheduled for December 2022.)

Predictably, the 1894 version of the Sluggers became otherworldly, with Fowler now playing full time in Findlay and Drake signing minor-league manager Charles Stroebel. The August 12, 1894 *Cleveland Press* reported the following:

> *Findlay's Great Team*
> *Findlay, O., Aug. 11—Spl—The Findlay ball team has played 59 games and has won 52. There is no other team in the country with such a record. The team is made up of as follows: Fowler 2b, Brandenburg rf, Johnson ss, Woods c, Cooke 3b, Ogden lf, Swartz cf, Derby 1b, Reidy and Pastorius pitchers. Reidy is a Cleveland boy and formerly played with the Albions.*

In September, the Brooklyn Bridegrooms league club stopped in town for an exhibition game and "found out just how good Finley was. They barely pulled out a 7–6 win." Days later, it was announced that Fowler and Johnson had struck a deal with a woven wire fence company located in Adrian, Michigan, to field a barnstorming, independent, all-Black team the following year, the Page Fence Giants.

By late September, the Findlay squad had conquered Ohio and the baseball firmament. The *Chicago Tribune* carried this article:

Findlay O. Sept. 29 [Special] *Findlay won the deciding game in this* [best of three game] *series with the Toledo in the Western League for the championship of Ohio outside the National League. Findlay has played 100 games this season and lost only 12. Nine games have been won over the Western League out of 12 games played.*
Findlay.............1 0 0 1 3 0 0 3 0—8.
Toledo.............0 0 1 0 0 1 1 0 0—3.
Batteries—Pastorious and Woods; Foreman and Berryhill, Hits—Findlay 9, Toledo 8. Errors—Findlay 5, Toledo 5. Home Runs—Pastorious and McFarland.

In 1895, Findlay's success led to their entry into the all-white Interstate League, minus Fowler and Home Run Johnson. They were both playing for the Page Fence Giants, possibly the greatest aggregate of baseball talent assembled to that time. When on the road, the Page Fence team took the rails, traveling in a special touring train car from destination to

The 1893 Findlay Sluggers with dapper NYPANOs alumni William Drake (1863–1919) (*standing, far right*), Youngstown catcher extraordinaire Bobby Wood (1865–1943) (*seated, front center, with catcher's mitt*) and African American great Grant "Home Run" Johnson (1872–1963) (*standing center*). *Thomas Drake.*

The 1894 edition of the Findlay Sluggers featured Hall of Famer Bud Fowler (*second row, seated far right*), Home Run Johnson (*second row, seated far left*) and Mahoning Valley native Bobby Wood (*second row, seated second from right, next to Fowler*). Famed Western author Zane Grey (1872–1939) later signed on with the 1895 edition of the Sluggers (along with his brother Reddy). *Thomas Drake.*

destination. The players soon proved to be masters of ballyhoo, riding bicycles en masse in their colorful uniforms to prospective whistle stops to hustle games against the local nine. The Page Fence Giants finished their fledgling season with a sparkling record of 118-36, a .766 winning percentage. Fowler, age thirty-seven, hit .316 for the year, exiting the team late in the season for a final stint with Lansing in the Michigan State League, batting .331 in what was to be his tenth and final season in organized baseball—a then record for longevity for an African American ballplayer. Ever the tumbleweed, Fowler uncharacteristically established a quasi-residence in "Flag City, USA" for the remainder of the decade, presumedly to align with William Drake, ever the visionary and about 150 years ahead of his time. Fowler's association with his former NYPANOs teammate became the most important chapter in his baseball life. As late as 1899, the two men were still trying to keep Fowler on the ball field, a task becoming increasingly impossible. White teammates would not take the field with him. The professional partnership with Fowler at an end, Drake on his own continued to promote baseball until a horrific accident at a hunting lodge on February 6, 1906, left him forever blind and paraplegic. Drake's infirmity ended forever Fowler's protracted journey across the diamond trails. He was at once a player nonpareil on the diamond and a true Renaissance man apart from the sport.

NILES NATIVE WILLIAM McKINLEY AND THE FIRST CELEBRITY PITCH

McKinley on Ball—The President a Lover of the National Game
—Sporting Life, *1897*

The decent work will go on. It cannot be stopped.…But who can tell the new thoughts that have been awakened, the ambition, fire and high achievements that will be rocked by this exposition?
—William McKinley's *final speech, September 5, 1901*

*I*n the aftermath of the nation's 1896 general election, newspaper scribes reported that president-elect and Mahoning Valley native William McKinley was an avid follower of baseball. In response, in his new town, the last-place Washington Senators promptly erected a "presidential" luxury box on the grandstand of Boundary Field, adjacent to the press box, allowing "the president to invite friends whenever he shall honor the park with his presence." To that end, Senators manager Gus Schmelz extended an invite to the president to throw out the ceremonial first pitch for the 1897 season, not unlike an event held five years earlier when McKinley, as Ohio governor, threw out the season-opening first pitch from the grandstand for a Columbus-Toledo game. Schmelz (who was a Columbus native) had arranged that earlier event as the manager of the Columbus Solons. When queried by the press about the throw, McKinley smiled at the memory and promised to make every effort to attend the festivities on April 22 at Boundary Field unless matters of an urgent nature intervened.

Alas, the opening event missed the mark on both fronts. As reported by the *Washington Post*, the twenty-fifth president was a no-show as the Senators lost to the Brooklyn Bridegrooms, 5–4. However, McKinley's earlier 1892 toss marked the first celebrity first pitch in the history of organized baseball and set a precedent that has continued to the present day. There is no record of the accuracy of the throw.

Born in Niles, Ohio, on January 29, 1843, William McKinley, schooled at Poland Academy and Allegheny College, was a teacher at a small country school when the Civil War broke out. Enlisting at age eighteen in the Union army with the Twenty-Third Ohio Volunteer Infantry, McKinley served under General Rutherford B. Hayes, who later became the nineteenth president of the United States (1876–80). On September 17, 1862, nineteen-year-old McKinley distinguished himself at the bloody Battle of Antietam. On his own initiative, he commandeered a wagon of supplies under enemy fire, "coaxed a few soldiers around him to help, and brought much-desired nourishment" to the "exhausted troops fighting near the Burnside Bridge." In a letter to his wife, Lucy, General Hayes had nothing but praise for the enterprising McKinley, describing him as "an exceedingly bright, intelligent, and gentlemanly young officer." By the end of the war, McKinley had risen in rank from a lowly private to brevet major. His final promotion, authorized by President Abraham Lincoln, was for meritorious service at the Battles of Fisher's Hill and Cedar Creek. McKinley became an attorney after the war. He set up a law practice in Canton, Ohio, and subsequently married Ida Saxon, the daughter of a local banker.

At age thirty-four, McKinley entered national politics as a Republican, winning a seat in the U.S. Congress. Once again, he rose quickly and served for years on the powerful Ways and Means Committee. During his fourteen years in the House of Representatives, the Ohio congressman unwaveringly sided with the public at large when proposed legislation was at odds with the often scurrilous and monopolistic private interests of the late nineteenth century. The ever-popular McKinley then served two terms as Ohio governor (January 11, 1892–January 13, 1896). In June 1896, with the former governor's political star still rising, Cleveland businessperson Mark Hanna offered McKinley's name as a candidate on the Republican ticket for the 1896 presidential nomination. McKinley handily defeated the Democratic nominee, William Jennings Bryan, to become the twenty-fifth U.S. president.

While McKinley promised prosperity on the homefront during his campaign; it was instead foreign affairs that dominated his first term in office. On the evening of February 15, 1898, the battleship USS *Maine* mysteriously blew up while docked at Havana, Cuba. The vessel had been dispatched to protect American interests as the Cuban colonial rebellion escalated into violence and civil war against their oppressive "landlords" in Spain. In the aftermath of the explosion, in which 260 American sailors lost their lives, journalistic license by major American newspapers inflamed public sentiment with sensationalistic "Remember the Maine!" headlines and propaganda. McKinley had little choice but to abandon his previous stance of neutrality in the conflict and declare war on Spain. The one-hundred-day Spanish-American War began on April 25, 1898, and ended on August 12 of that year. It was a total victory for America both on land and at sea and achieved the independence of Cuba. The United States acquired the territories of Guam and Puerto Rico in the aftermath of the war. Theodore "Teddy" Roosevelt, who famously led his hearty band of Rough Riders to victory on San Juan Hill, became at once a national hero in the "yellow" press and McKinley's vice-presidential running mate in the election of 1900 in what proved to be a rematch and a veritable landslide victory against their Democrat opponent, William Jennings Bryan.

On September 5, 1901, President McKinley formally spoke for about two and a half minutes at the Pan-American Exposition in Buffalo, New York, as motion-picture cameras silently recorded the event for posterity. The president delivered his remarks on a large outdoor wooden podium framed overhead with six draped, oversized American flags. An estimated fifty thousand people attended the event. In the vast crowd was a twenty-eight-year-old anarchist named Leon Czolgosz (pronounced "Sholgosh") carrying a concealed pistol with murder on his mind. And although Czolgosz managed to get close to the president, the would-be assassin did not fire his weapon that day due to the uncertainty caused by the large assemblage. He had fallen on tough times during and after the Great Panic of 1893 and regarded McKinley as a symbol of oppression.

The following day, the president attended a "meet and greet" event at the exposition's Temple of Music building, despite the heated objections of his secretary, George B. Cortelyou, who had real safety concerns. As McKinley shook hands with well-wishers, he encountered Czolgosz, who shot the president twice in the abdomen at point-blank range. McKinley collapsed, mortally wounded. The assassin was immediately arrested by the Secret Service. President William McKinley died of gangrene on September 14, 1901, nine days after he was shot. He was fifty-eight years old. His last words were: "God's will be done, not ours." With the president's demise, Czolgosz's

Left: William McKinley (1843–1901) was born in Niles, Ohio. The future president lived in the Mahoning Valley until his ninth birthday. He was one of nine children. After his death, McKinley's birth home was restored to its original condition by a wealthy attorney from Warren, Ohio, Lulu McKay, after being relocated to her two-hundred-acre estate at Tibbets Corners (later renamed McKinley Heights). On April 3, 1937, the house burned to the ground. *Niles Historical Society.*

Right: McKinley Memorial Foundation certificate hand signed by Joseph G. Butler Jr. (1840–1927). The library/museum opened on October 5, 1917. Butler had been the boyhood and lifelong friend of William McKinley. Butler was instrumental in promoting and obtaining funding for the National McKinley Memorial after the president's 1901 assassination. *Author's collection.*

fate was a forgone conclusion. Sentenced to death at trial, the assassin was executed by electrocution on October 29, 1901. To the end, the anarchist had no remorse or regret for his crime.

Present-day historians have mixed assessments of the effectiveness of McKinley's presidency, but none can dispute the simple fact that he remained enormously popular throughout his political career. There is no better testimonial to his memory than the final words of what was to be his final speech: "Gentlemen, let us ever remember that our interest is in concord, not conflict; that our real eminence rests in the victories of peace and not in the goals of war."

"MIRACLE MAN"
JOHN D. "BONESETTER" REESE

Who has made his home in Youngstown and was famed in all the zones
as Mr.-Man-Who-Beat-the-World-at-Setting-Broken-Bones?
Who got the job when Tyrus Cobb, the score an aching void,
slid forty feet to save the game and snapped his sesamoid?
Who answered Babe Ruth's call for help amid mad fans Hoorah,
when, dashing for a fly he tripped and snapped his fibula?
Who proved to be Pep Martin's friend and straightened out his thumb,
when someone's in shoot pegged him right on his trapezium?
Whose worldwide fame might still have shown phenomenal
increase could he have cured bone headedness?
—*Anonymous,* Sioux City Journal

Every time a baseball player gets a kink in his wing the announcement is expected
that he has gone to Youngstown O., for treatment in the hands of bonesetter Reese.
This man had done more than any other to put Youngsville—er—town on the
baseball map.
—Wilkes-Barre Record

Through six decades, he had the healing touch, his tactile skill and physical mechanics the stuff of legend. Known as the "Miracle Man," John D. Reese was the bone-setting orthopedic manipulator for the Mahoning Valley, baseball and the world at large. Born on May 6, 1855, in Rhymey, Wales, Reese was orphaned at ten and subsequently forced to work at the town's local ironworks. The boy was soon after taken in by local resident Tom Jones and his family. Jones, a childless coworker, taught the youth the long-standing tradition of Welsh bone setting used primarily for the treatment of strains in muscles and tendons for the "mountain people" of Wales. The technique was also used, less frequently, for the actual setting of bone fractures.

During his long apprenticeship with Jones, Reese displayed a remarkable natural ability for the arcane science of bone setting, which combines the art of the chiropractor with the physical elements of the osteopath. He did not require the use of X-rays for treatment. In his later years, Reese was unable to fully "explain his abnormally developed sense of touch, the secret of his successful diagnosis of cases that…puzzled train surgeons. It was a gift of nature, one of those strange psychological phenomena that defies the rules of the exact science of surgery.…For the rest, Reese [claimed] nothing more than a mere knowledge of anatomy derived from close study and reading and the keen insight into that requirement of the case together with the natural strength of arm and hand necessary to apply the cure" (*Philadelphia Enquirer*, January 12, 1913).

Reese immigrated to the United States in 1887 and applied his bone-setting skills part time to Mahoning Valley residents in the brief off-hours while he worked from dawn to dusk as a puddler at the Brown Bonnell Mills in Youngstown, Ohio. A brief time after Reese's arrival, a fellow millworker who had been seriously injured after falling off a ladder was "straightened out," completely healed with Reese's unique physiotherapies. The incident resulted in a steady stream of local business for Reese alleviating pain and curing the infirm. The bonesetter, in June 1894, set up professionally. The rest is history. Reese treated as many as eighty patients a day and accepted whatever the patient could afford. Many of his poor, working-class clientele were healed free of charge, their discarded crutches left behind as payment. Reese's only "formal" medical training was a one-time, intensive, three-week anatomy study at Ohio State University.

Bonesetter Reese became known to the world when his manipulative treatment instantaneously healed ailing Cleveland Spiders hurler "Nig" Cuppy's sensitive pitching wing in 1897. "There are two cords out of place, but I can set them," Reese declared after a quick examination. After a few painful twists and turns of the arm and shoulder, Cuppy walked out a new man. Jimmy McAleer, who was himself cured by the bonesetter in 1894, had recommended Reese to Cuppy. The *Brooklyn Daily Eagle* stated: "The national and widely international fame that followed…is due to his treatment of ballplayers…who became multitudinous press agents for Bonesetter Reese and the newspaper writers gladly spread the tidings."

The *Daily Eagle* continued:

> *What almost invariably astonishes ballplayer patients and presumably others is that Doctor Reese seldom…works…his treatment in the place where they feel the pain.…Ed Reulbach who helped pitch Brooklyn to the pennant in 1916…acquired some trouble in the back of his right leg that crippled…his running and pitching.…Reulbach visited Bonesetter Reese and gave him an earful of his troubles. Bonesetter told him to lie on the examination table face downward. Dr. Reese then astonished Reulbach beyond words by paying no attention at all to his leg but by nearly breaking his back with a series of knuckle pushes, varied now and then by a terrific gripping.*
>
> *Reulbach said afterward that he thought he was being murdered but all of the sudden the Bonesetter ceased and told him to make room for another patient. The player's back was still sore from the rough but necessary treatment, but he noticed the change for the better in his leg as soon as he rose to his feet. He was pitching as well as ever in a few days and was never bothered with his leg again.*

Over time, Reese treated scores of athletes both amateur and professional and "saved enough of them to equip a major league." Reese's agile therapies served as a conduit to link forever many of the best players of the era to the Mahoning Valley, including six of the ten players initially enshrined at Cooperstown. Among the Hall of Famers Reese cured at his 219 Park Avenue home office were: Babe Ruth, Rogers Hornsby, Ty Cobb, Christy Mathewson, Honus Wagner, Red Ruffing, Fred Clark, Home Run Baker, Napoleon Lajoie, Rube Marquard, Cy Young, Burleigh Grimes, Bobby Wallace, Ed Walsh and Stan Coveleski. Other players cured include pitchers Reulbach, Cleveland's Cuppy, George Uhle, Benny Karr, Glenn Wright and Earl Moore, Warrenite Leon "Red" Ames, Sherrod Smith, Marty O'Toole, Hooks Wiltse, George Mullen, Barney Pelty, "Long" Tom Hughes, Frank Lange, Niles native Pat Griffin, Howie Camnitz, Orvie Overall, Doc Scanlon, Louis Drucke and Patsy Flaherty. Position players include McAleer, Tommy Leach, Kid Elberfeld, Kitty Bransfield, Naps player Terry Turner, Bris Lord, Billy Sullivan, Pepper Martin, Patsy Dougherty, George McBride, Del Gainer, Sherry McGee, Charlie Eagle Eye Hemphill, Doc Gessler and future mass murderer Marty Bergen.

Reese also successfully treated American president Theodore Roosevelt; Chief Justice Charles Evans Hughes; famed boxing champions Gene Tunney, Battling Nelson and Cleveland's Johnny Kilbane; famed comedian Will Rogers; British political leader David Lloyd George; actor Pat Rooney; Broadway and film star Fred Stone; and Youngstown-born vaudeville and stage actress/comedienne Rae Samuels.

For a time, Reese's most celebrated patient was a horse, following the successful 1901 treatment of it by Reese. The horse, Lord Vincent, was once owned by wealthy Valley resident George Tod. The famous Youngstown Thoroughbred trotter had pulled lame just two years after winning the 1899 $10,000 Transylvania Stakes in Lexington, Kentucky, and the $10,000 Charter Oak Stakes the same year. Reese received a second dose of publicity for this amazing remedy in 1902, when a second worldwide wave of newspaper articles corrected some erroneous initial reporting that the Christian Science chapter of Youngstown was responsible for the horse's stunning cure.

Perhaps Reese's two most miraculous treatments (of humans) happened over the course of twenty-seven years. On November 20, 1896, the bonesetter successfully treated twelve-year-old Wayne Barnham, who pridefully walked out of Reese's office after an injury had hobbled him for three years. Numerous prior visits to an array of doctors often of worldwide repute had proven fruitless. After a brief treatment by Reese, the boy walked out, his discarded crutches added to the bonesetter's ever-growing collection. Years later, on April 13, 1923, Niles youngster B.F. Pew, who was totally paralyzed on the left side and unable to be moved, received a rare home visit from Reese at his Emma Street address. "The Welshman's deft fingers roamed across the boy's shoulders, suddenly he pressed upon something, a bone snapped into place and the boy walked." Such tales had by then become routine.

Reese's most personally lucrative treatment came rather late in his career. In 1928, the Cleveland billionaires and real estate and railroad magnates the Van Sweringen brothers, Oris and Mantis, who were at that time among the principal shareholders of the Cleveland Indians, desired Reese to treat their accumulated aches and pains at their palatial estate in Shaker Heights, near downtown Cleveland. Reese's busy practice did not permit the sixty-mile rail journey and the Bonesetter politely declined their request. He could easily treat them in his Youngstown office. The Van Swearingen pair were morbidly reclusive and equally persistent, finally negotiating for Reese's one-night courtesy stay at their new Terminal

Tower in downtown Cleveland, plus a retainer of $1,000 for the home visit (the equivalent of $15,998.10 today).

Reese was not the first to practice the fine art of bone setting on the North American continent. In 1630, Welsh émigré John Sweet arrived in Plymouth, Massachusetts. Sweet applied his orthopedic bone-setting skills to treat local farmers and shopkeepers and commenced the family tradition of passing down the knowledge, in his case to the ablest of his sons. And it was fifth-generation practitioner Dr. Job Sweet whose orthopedic manipulation and phenomenally comforting bedside manner affected many cures during the carnage of the Revolutionary War. His successful postwar treatment of Theodosia Burr, the teenage daughter of Aaron Burr, the vice president under Thomas Jefferson, brought both national and international fame to the practice of bone setting and the preternatural skills of Sweet, by then a septuagenarian. The Sweet family continued their practice through four centuries.

Dr. John D. Reese died of massive coronary thrombosis at the age of seventy-six on November 30, 1931, at his Park Ave home in Youngstown. Bonesetter Reese had suffered a severe heart attack earlier that year and was at the time effectively in retirement. Five daughters survived Reese. At the time of his death, Reese was a thirty-second-degree Scottish Rite Mason, a Knight Templar and a life member of the Al Koran Temple in Cleveland. In the years before his death, Reese's physical appearance resembled that of the elderly Mark Twain, with a billowy white mustache, which starkly set apart his deep blue eyes. At his funeral, the 1883 John H. Herman hymn "Lead Kindly Light" was featured, sung by local talent Mary Novella Jones Freed. An excerpt follows:

> *Lead kindly Light amid th' encircling gloom,*
> *Lead thou me on;…*
> *So long Thy pow'r has blest me, sure it still.*
> *Wilt lead me on,*
> *O'er moor and fen,*
> *O'er crag and torrent, till*
> *The night is gone,*
> *And with the morn those angel faces smile,*
> *Which I have loved long since and lost awhile.*

Left: "Bonesetter" John Reese (1855–1931), world-famous master of orthopedics and the subject of a Pathe newsreel documentary, *He Tells What Ails Them*. *Mahoning Valley Historical Society*.

Below: John Reese was the rightfully proud owner of a brand-new 1919 Cadillac with all the "bells and whistles." Moments after this photo was snapped, Reese was cited for violating a city no-parking zone. *Mahoning Valley Historical Society*.

Bonesetter Reese patients Benny Karr (1893–1968) (*left*) and George Uhle (1898–1985). *Cleveland Press Collection*.

POSTSCRIPT

Aaron Burr is most notorious for killing his political rival, Treasury Secretary Alexander Hamilton, with a pistol in a staged but nonetheless illegal duel to the death. He was never tried. Burr was later acquitted of the charge of treason in a sensational trial after attempting to insert himself as the president of Mexico during a time of political upheaval in that country. The ensuing scandal ended forever his illustrious political career in the United States.

His daughter Theodosia later married and became the most celebrated American socialite of the time. On December 31, 1812, Theodosia boarded the *Patriot*, a small schooner bound for New York City. The vessel was lost at sea, likely the victim of pirates operating within the Outer Banks region of North Carolina.

CY YOUNG, ED McKEAN, JIMMY McALEER, NIG CUPPY, BOBBY WALLACE AND THE 1895 TEMPLE CUP CHAMPIONS

A robust specimen of the genus homo is Young. The world at large has never known what name was saddled on Cy at the baptismal font.
—Chicago Tribune, *August 13, 1892*

Young lets the ball go as though he were about to push it down about [the batters'] *unprotected heads. If I had Young, I'd win the championship in a walk.*
—Cap Anson, *Chicago Cubs player-manager*

Hurrah for the pennant winners!
Hurrah for Captain Tebeau!
Hurrah for the plucky baseball management.
—Cleveland Leader, *October 12, 1892*

The greatest pitchers' duel of the nineteenth century was the first game of the postseason matchup for the 1892 Temple Cup crown between future Hall of Fame hurler Cy Young, who had won thirty-six games for the Cleveland Spiders that year, and Jack Stivetts, a thirty-five-game winner for the Boston Beaneaters. Both men had worked over 400 innings. With the National League once again a monopoly, expanded to twelve teams, through an absorption of four ballclubs from the newly defunct American Association, the 1892 season had been split into two halves: the team with the best record in the spring would play the winner of the fall schedule in a best-of-nine-game World Series. Boston won in the spring, with a record of 52-22. Cleveland, meanwhile, had finished fifth (40–33) in the first half but caught fire down the stretch after obtaining Boston's disgruntled pitching ace and future Hall of Famer John Clarkson, who contributed seventeen important wins in the last weeks of the season as the Spiders finished the second half with a record of 50-23 for a .697 winning percentage, three games ahead of the Beaneaters. Player-manager Patsy Tebeau (pronounced "Tebow") succeeded in molding the Cleveland ball club in his own image: a scrappy, hard-fighting unit that played full tempo until the final out. Tebeau's crew was hard to a man and ready and willing to use their fists if necessary to intimidate opponents and umpires alike. Youngstown alumni shortstop Ed McKean recorded a team high ninety-three RBIs that year, and Valley native center fielder Jimmy McAleer scored 92 runs. McKean's double-play partner, second baseman Cupid Childs, scored a league-high 136 runs. Future Hall of Famer George Davis played third base but was versatile enough to fill any position. Outfielder Jesse Burkett was starting to find his way into Cooperstown with his bat. Rookie right-handed slow-baller Nig Cuppy won a career-high twenty-eight games. And, as incredible as it was for long-suffering Cleveland fans, the Spiders reached the postseason in its sixth season of operation.

The Temple Cup opener took place on October 17, 1892, at Cleveland's League Park. Game time was 3:00 p.m. sharp. The afternoon was warm, sunny, cloudless and unseasonably warm, a perfect backdrop for a historic event. The pennant-starved Cleveland "cranks" came out in droves, as over six thousand people crammed every available seat at the park. The umpires were Bo Emslie and Snyder. The nail-biting contest between two of the best hurlers in baseball did not disappoint. From the beginning, the game "was, above all and everything a pitcher's battle. The stout, well-seasoned bats that had helped both Cleveland and Boston onto many a victory were powerless when opposed to the ball scurrying through space with the swiftness of a meteor or writhing and twisting like a mammoth snake as its curves carried it one way or another."

Inning after inning, the goose eggs piled up for both teams. Finally, in the Cleveland ninth, things got interesting. With one out, Jesse Burkett laid down a perfect bunt down the third-base line that "finally hit the bag for a single. [George] Davis' hard smash at…the Boston first baseman handcuffed him, and Davis beat it out for a hit." McKean followed with a hard grounder to Joe Quinn at second that forced out Davis for the second out as Burkett held at third and McKean reached first. Quinn felt that Davis had interfered with his chance at a double play. "While he was arguing, Burkett was edging off third, and suddenly made a dash for the plate. Quinn recovered his wits just in time.…A foot farther and Burkett would have won the game for Cleveland." After that scare, both pitchers doubled down. After three hours of play and with twilight descending, the umpires had no choice but to call the game. The greatest-pitched game at that point in history ended with a 0–0 tie after twelve innings.

Boston won every remaining game of the series to rightfully claim the world championship. Ed McKean batted .440 in postseason play and recorded six RBIs. Cupid Childs batted .409; Jesse Burkett hit .320. Pitcher John Clarkson blasted the only home run for either team. But the Spiders, even in defeat, had shown they could play with the best.

The history of the new Cleveland franchise began just three years after the Blue Stockings' ignominious exit from the National League at the end of the 1884 season. A consortium of wealthy Cleveland businesspeople led by streetcar magnates Frank and Stanley Robison and Davis Hawley pooled their financial resources to successfully put together another team, resurrecting the Blues name, along with two former Blue Stockings stars, center fielder Pete Hotaling and Hugh "One Arm" Daily. The team entered the American Association in 1887 and played at Association Park, built on the dead ends of Thirty-Sixth Street and Perkins Avenue. The hitting star of the new team was the former Youngstown infielder Ed McKean, who batted .286 in his MLB debut. The team finished last but had nowhere to go but up. And in 1888, the team rose to sixth place in the American Association standings.

Cleveland rejoined the National League the next season with a new name, the Spiders. The team added McKean's Y'town teammate Jimmy McAleer to the roster (and, for one season, Youngstown native Deacon McGuire). McAleer's defensive prowess utterly transformed the franchise, as the speedster proved to be a one-man outfield. Meanwhile, the power-hitting McKean was increasingly revolutionizing the offensive output at the shortstop position, finishing fifth that year in home runs and fourth in on-base average (OBA). And although the team repeated their sixth-place season finish, it was in the much stronger National League. The Spiders' talent pool would receive a huge boost the next year with the late-season signing of Cy Young, the greatest pitcher in baseball history and a player with distinct ties to the Mahoning Valley, due to his association with Bonesetter Reese, who extended his twenty-two-year MLB career.

Young's signing came about in the aftermath of actions by Cleveland's streetcar tycoon, Al Johnson. Johnson utilized a "workers united" platform to siphon off many of the game's biggest stars in order to form a rival league,

Players League, in 1890. Nearly all of Cleveland's major stars, including Jimmy McAleer, jumped to the new league. Ed McKean was one of only two players who remained with the parent club. Johnson controversially decided to go head-to-head with the best and biggest teams in all the major cities from the National League and the American Association. As a result, attendance for ball teams in all three leagues fell precipitously, the result of the glut in the baseball marketplace. Fans were divided in their patronage, and all the franchises lost money. Meanwhile, MLB teams were scrambling during the season to sign undiscovered talent to fill the holes in their rosters, as many prominent players had jumped to the Players League. In hindsight, this was the scenario that led to the late-season signing of the burly, twenty-three-year-old farmer from Tuscarawas County, Ohio, Cy Young. He was preternaturally strong, with a decidedly rural temperament that masked a powerful desire to make good in the baseball world.

Denton True Young, born in Gilmore, Ohio, on March 29, 1867, had been scouted as a third baseman and passed by in 1889. He was subsequently invited to try out as a pitcher for the lowly and desperate Canton Nadjys in the Tri-State League the following year. Young, full of ambition, was determined to make a good showing: "All of us Youngs could throw. I used to kill squirrels with a stone as a kid and my granddad once killed a turkey buzzard on the fly with a rock." During his Canton audition, Young held nothing back, throwing full-out with abandon. Working without a catcher, the soon-to-be ex-farmer utterly shattered the slats of the wooden backstop. The splintered wood looked as if it had been struck by an earthquake. Or a cyclone. The awestruck Canton manager signed him on the spot. Denton Young's moniker was forever changed to "Cy."

Cy Young pitched very well for the Nadjys and in September threw a no-hitter against McKeesport, Pennsylvania, striking out eighteen batters. Shortly after, Cleveland Spiders traveling secretary Davis Hawley came calling and signed the twenty-three-year-old phenom for $500. The Spiders, anxious to see their new addition, threw Young against Cap Anson's Chicago Cubs before an appropriately sized uniform could be ordered. Young took the field in an ill-fitting uniform several sizes too small for his frame. Young quickly became the object of ridicule against Anson's worldly veterans. Young angrily defeated Chicago, allowing catcher Chief Zimmer to call the pitches. After the game, Anson offered Hawley $1,000 for Young's services. The offer was summarily declined. Young won nine games in his first foray in the major leagues and spent the off-season strengthening his arm by splitting rails on his father's farm. Apart from his preternatural strength and durability, the raw-boned Young carefully studied opposition batters and had a photographic memory of their strengths and weaknesses.

In 1891, the Robisons opened a new stadium, League Park. It was built on their streetcar line on East Sixty-Sixth Street, Lexington Avenue, Beecher Avenue (later Linwood) and East Seventieth. It had a capacity of nine thousand, and its dimensions were 375 feet to the left-field wall, 420 feet to dead center and 240 feet to right, a result of the configuration of the urban streets and housing. The stadium was a venue worthy of the team's new phenomenon. The Spiders named Patsy Tebeau as the manager at midseason, and Young posted twenty-seven victories. The Spiders finished fifth with a record of 65-74.

The 1892 addition of future Hall of Fame outfielder Jesse Burkett and two pitchers—rookie Nig Cuppy and veteran John Clarkson—to the Spiders roster paid immediate dividends. Cleveland reached the postseason for the first time in the city's history, posting an overall record of 84-48. The next year, after their defeat for the Temple Cup crown, the Spiders traded for Hall of Famer Buck Ewing, giving up George Davis. The move netted the team third place in the standings, with a 73-55 record. On paper, the Ewing-Davis trade was one Hall of Famer for another. But Ewing was in the sere and yellow of his long career, while Davis improved with age and would continue his road to Cooperstown for another decade. In 1894, personnel issues with Buck Ewing and John Clarkson poisoned the clubhouse camaraderie. Both exited the team that year, and the Spiders fell further in the standings amid the turmoil.

Then came 1895.

The Baltimore Orioles had replaced the Boston Beaneaters and Cap Anson's Chicago Cubs with the strongest starting lineup in the majors, one populated with five Hall of Famers: right fielder Willie Keeler, shortstop Hughie Jennings (who would later coach Valley great Billy Evans), left fielder Joe Kelley, catcher Wilbert Robinson and third baseman John McGraw. Baltimore won the pennant race in 1894 for their first championship but was shut out in the Temple Cup series, losing four games to New York. In 1895, the Orioles introduced Bill Hoffer (pronounced "Hoe-fer"), who broke into the majors in a big way with a record of 31-6. Six Orioles batted above .300, and the team won eighty-seven games.

Meanwhile, Spiders ace Cy Young suffered a rare arm injury to start the season. He did not pitch his first game until April 28. Despite missing at least two starts, Young put together one of the finest seasons, leading the league in wins (thirty-five) and possessing the lowest opposition on-base percentage.

Nig Cuppy won twenty-eight games, and versatile newcomer Bobby Wallace added another eleven. Wallace later morphed into a shortstop and reached the Hall of Fame in 1953.

In 1895, everything seemed to go the Spiders' way, as Jesse Burkett led the league with a staggering .426 batting average. Not surprisingly, he also topped the league in hits (225). Bonesetter Reese patients Cy Young, Nig Cuppy and Bobby Wallace made up the pitching staff. Youngstown alumni shortstop Ed McKean had a season for the ages at his position, leading all players in at bats while blasting a whopping 119 RBIs. Even Jimmy McAleer had career year, batting .277. The Spiders won eighty-four games and earned the right to play Baltimore for the Temple Cup in a best-of-seven series. The first three contests were to be played in Cleveland, with the next three in Baltimore. Cleveland would host a seventh game if required.

GAME ONE: BALTIMORE ORIOLES AT CLEVELAND SPIDERS, WEDNESDAY, OCTOBER 2, 1895

"The gates at League Park registered 7,000 People for game one of the Temple Cup Championship series. The enthusiasm vent in noises of all conceivable varieties, fish horns, whistles, rattles, and plain but strenuous voices being in the ascendancy" (*Cleveland Press*, October 3, 1895).

Pitchers Cy Young for the Spiders and Sadie McMahon for the Orioles pitched scoreless ball for four frames. In the fifth, the batters for both teams took over, and the game became an offensive battle. Spiders third baseman Chippy McGarr got things started when he singled to left. Next up was pitcher Young, who beat out a bunt. Jesse Burkett then advanced both runners with a sacrifice. Youngstown alumni Ed McKean hit a long fly out to right. McGarr was able to tag up and beat the throw home for the first run of the series. Baltimore came right back in the next frame. John McGraw singled and later scored to tie the game. In the bottom of the sixth, Tebeau hit a daisy-cutter single and advanced when the slow-running catcher Zimmer narrowly beat out a hit. Next, Harry Blake hit a deep dive to the center-field wall. Tebeau scored easily, but Zimmer held at third, unsure if he could beat the throw home. The inning ended with Cleveland back on top, 2–1. The seventh inning was scoreless.

In the eighth, McGraw and Jennings scored, but Cleveland came back to tie the game, 3–3, when Jesse Burkett doubled and later scored on Ed McKean's sac fly.

Then came the ninth.

The Orioles came back against Young, as Hall of Fame catcher Wilbert Robinson doubled and later scored on John McGraw's double to go ahead, 4–3.

It was dusk when the Spiders came to bat. Burkett started things off with a double. McKean wasted no time lining a shot past shortstop Keeler as Burkett raced home to tie the score. Cupid Childs and McAleer both singled to load the bases with no outs. Manager Tebeau's grounder forced McKean at the plate. Bases were still loaded with one out. Catcher Zimmer slapped another grounder, forcing Tebeau at second, but Zimmer beat the throw to first as Childs crossed the plate for the winning run. The Spiders won, 5–4.

GAME TWO: BALTIMORE ORIOLES AT CLEVELAND SPIDERS, THURSDAY, OCTOBER 3, 1895

The crowd at League Park was estimated at between eight thousand and ten thousand. Some of the fans were "overly enthusiastic," throwing seat cushions, beer bottles and whistles at the visitors. No one was hurt in the mêlée. The pitchers for this game were Nig Cuppy for Cleveland and Bill Hoffer of Baltimore.

Cuppy was the hitting and pitching star, throwing a five-hitter and doubling home a run despite being bloodied in the second frame by a line drive. The Spiders won, 7–2. Jesse Burkett had a double and three singles as the Spiders outplayed Baltimore at every turn. Burkett, McKean, Childs, McAleer, Tebeau, Zimmer and Cuppy scored for the Spiders. Jennings and Kelly scored for Baltimore.

GAME THREE: BALTIMORE ORIOLES AT CLEVELAND SPIDERS, SATURDAY, OCTOBER 5, 1895

A record twelve thousand fans filled every "nook and cranny, perched on fences and ringed the outfield" at Cleveland's League Park. Because of the presence of fans in the outfield, there were special ground rules: all fair balls into the crowd would be scored as doubles. The day was bright and sunny with a tinge of autumnal cool in the air. The pitchers were Cy Young and Sadie McMahon. The overflow crowd was orderly, perhaps because of the total dominance of the Spiders in every aspect of the game. Young did not let a ball past the infield until the ninth. The Spiders' batters did not strand a single runner for the entire game, and Young notched his second victory with a 7–1 triumph. McKean, Childs, McAleer, Zimmer, Blake, McGarr and Young scored. The game took one hour and forty-five minutes. Jim McDonald and Tim Hurst were the umpires.

GAME FOUR: CLEVELAND SPIDERS AT BALTIMORE ORIOLES, MONDAY, OCTOBER 7, 1895

For game four, the series moved to Baltimore. The pitchers were Nig Cuppy for Cleveland and southpaw Duke Esper for Baltimore. A large crowd of ten thousand fans pass through the turnstiles at Union Park. Due to the rumor of retaliatory violence against the visitors, there was a strong police presence during the game. But there were no incidents at the ballpark.

Cleveland manager Tebeau was supremely confident of a sweep and advised the Spiders to bring just "one shirt," as they wouldn't need more. But Baltimore pitcher Duke Esper, who was just 10-12 for the year, had always been a bane for Cleveland. This day was no exception. Esper was nothing short of brilliant, pitching a five-hit shutout as Baltimore dominated Cleveland in a 5–0 victory. Baltimore's Willie Keeler scored twice, and John McGraw, Hughie Jennings and centerfielder Steve Brodie each tallied once. So effortless was the Orioles' win that most Baltimoreans who exited the ballpark were convinced that their team would sweep at Union Park, resulting in a seventh game at Cleveland.

As they exited the ballpark to return to the Carrollton Hotel, the Spiders ballplayers were savagely accosted by a large, hostile crowd and pelted with sticks and rocks. The Cleveland players quickly flattened themselves on the omnibus floor and seats as the attack continued. Three miscreants were arrested at the scene.

GAME FIVE: CLEVELAND SPIDERS AT BALTIMORE ORIOLES, TUESDAY, OCTOBER 8, 1895

Due to the cold weather, attendance was down for this game, with estimates ranging between five thousand and nine thousand fans at Union Park. The pitchers were the two best hurlers of 1895: Cy Young for Cleveland and Bill Hoffer for Baltimore. In 1901, Hoffer would pitch the first opening game

Left: Cy Young (1867–1955) of the Cleveland Spiders. Young was one of the many players who had his baseball career extended by Youngstown's Bonesetter Reese. He maximized the extra time. Throughout his twenty-two-year career, Young won 511 games to establish the all-time wins record. *Author's collection*.

Below: The 1892 edition of the Cleveland Spiders reached postseason play for the first time. Players with ties to the Mahoning Valley were Ed McKean (1864–1919) (*kneeling, far right*), Jimmy McAleer (1864–1931) (*standing, third from right*), "Nig" Cuppy (1869–1922) (*kneeling, third from left*) and Cy Young (1867–1955) (*standing, far left*). Young, Jessie Burkett (1868–1953) (*kneeling, second from right*) and George Davis (1870–1940) (*standing, second from left*) have been inducted into the National Baseball Hall of Fame. *Cleveland Public Library*.

CLEVELAND BASE BALL CLUB OF 1892

in Cleveland Indians history. Young, meanwhile, would eventually become the winningest pitcher in Cleveland's MLB history, winning 240 games for the Spiders in the National League and, later, recording an additional 29 with the American League Indians. Young's 269 total victories for the city surpasses by 3 games another pitcher with peripheral ties to the Mahoning Valley: first-ballot Hall of Famer Bob Feller, who won 266 contests for the Indians/Guardians franchise.

On this day, Young and Hoffer dominated through six frames, trading goose eggs. It was Young himself who broke open the floodgates for Cleveland with a blistering two-baser that rolled into the shadow of the center-field scoreboard. Young advanced to third on Jesse Burkett's loud single and later scored, one of the Spiders' three runs in the seventh. Cleveland added two more runs in the eighth, with pitcher Young tallying twice. The Orioles worked a run in the home half of the inning.

Cy Young took a 5–1 lead into the final inning. He quickly retired the first two batters before issuing passes to John McGraw and Hughie Jennings. Clutch-hitting Joe Kelley then strode to the plate amid thunderous applause. He then hit a scratch single to score McGraw. There were two outs and two men on. Union Park became a madhouse as the next batter, outfielder Steve Brodie, hit a weak squib to Young for the final out. Cleveland had won the game, 5–2, and the Temple Cup championship—the first for the city.

Cleveland and Baltimore faced off again for the 1896 Temple Cup, Cleveland's third postseason appearance in five years. Baltimore swept the Spiders that year, four victories to none. The Cleveland Spiders never meaningfully contended for another championship. In 1897, the team morphed into the Indians for the first half of the season. The Indians saw sterling play by their new addition, Penobscot Indian Lou Sockalexis. Sockalexis succumbed to acute alcoholism, unable even to finish the 1897 season. The Cleveland team was decimated in 1899, when Cy Young and the entire Spiders club was transferred to St. Louis in an austerity move. The tattered Spiders, populated by castoffs culled from other teams, managed to win only twenty games during the season, the worst record in baseball history. The team was mercifully cut from the league at the conclusion of the season.

Cleveland professional baseball was resurrected in the newly formed American League in 1901. Its grand journey through history continues to the present day.

HARRY M. STEVENS,
THE "COSMOPOLITAN CONCESSIONAIRE"

Harry M. Stevens is a cosmopolitan figure. His regional genius and splendid energy has bought him wealth in numerous ventures and a large share has been invested to promote the welfare of his city.
—*Joseph G. Butler Jr.*

[Stevens] *died without ever having anyone say of him he cheated me.*
—*Quinton Reynolds*

The date: July 4, 2007. The most highly anticipated matchup in major-league eating history ended with San Jose State student Joey Chestnut winning the coveted Yellow Mustard Belt over Japanese rival Takeru Kobayashi in the ninety-second annual frankfurter-eating contest held at Nathan's Famous Hot Dog stand at Coney Island, New York. Suffering from a serious jaw injury, Kobayashi's participation in the event was in question until the last moments. A spillover crowd of fifty thousand watched the American's upset victory over the six-time former champion by downing sixty-six HDBs (hot dogs and buns) in twelve minutes, establishing a new record and bringing the title back to the United States, in the city where it all began.

Although frankfurters were first sold at the 1904 World's Fair in St. Louis Missouri, America's love affair with hot dogs dates to two years later, when Niles, Ohio concessionaire Harry M. Stevens introduced the fare during a 1906 New York Giants baseball game. Unusually chilly weather at the Polo Grounds prompted the Mahoning Valley resident to order an

Harry Mozely Stevens (1855–1934), pioneer promoter of the hot dog, the drinking straw and the scorecard. *Author's collection.*

emergency change in menu, from ice cream to the ethnic German sausages sold by itinerant street vendors neighboring the ballpark. The borrowed sandwich proved to be a sensation. In attendance that day was *New York Journal* cartoonist T.A. Dorgan, who drew Stevens's brainchild as a dachshund barking in a bun. Unsure of the spelling, Dorgan went back to the basics and captioned the item "hot dogs." (In addition to the hot dog, cartoonist Dorgan introduced into the lexicon "hard-boiled," "malarkey" and "kibitzer.") From these humble beginnings, the popularity of the frankfurter has become a staple at ballparks and barbecues across America and is considered one of summer's most symbolic food choices.

Born in England in 1855, Harry Mozley Stevens and his wife, Mary Wragg Stevens, immigrated to Niles, Ohio, in 1882 with just $5.00 to their name. Harry's arrival in the Valley was fortuitous. In Great Britain, he had heard glorious tales of good-paying, steady work in the iron and steel industry in a town called Niles. When Stevens reached the train station in New York City, he told the ticketmaster his destination. He was asked, "Ohio or Michigan?" The rest is history. Stevens took a job as a puddler in the local Ward steel mills until his job evaporated on Black Friday 1883. To make ends meet for a growing family, Stevens changed vocations from puddler to peddler, taking a job selling door to door, initially hawking a book written by General John J. Logan called *The Great Conspiracy* for an agency headquartered in Columbus. (John Logan was a rambunctious member of Congress, a general in the course of Sherman's fiery march through Georgia and the founder of Memorial Day.) Stevens became a nomad of salesmanship but continued to maintain his primary residence in the Mahoning Valley. Due to his unbridled success as a bookseller, in 1887, Stevens, with just $8.40 in his pocket, purchased the rights "to publish and peddle" the minor-league Columbus Buckeyes' nickel scorecard enterprise for $500. And within twenty-four hours, "he had hustled advertisers to the tune of $700." Stevens sold the

A Depression-era Harry Stevens program from Cleveland's League Park, dated Sunday, June 21, 1936, lavishly scored in red ink. One of the ancillary benefits of Stevens's brainchild is that it remains a veritable time capsule of a moment in history. Depression-era dollars were dear for many baseball fans. Quite often, a Harry Stevens Stahl Meyer hot dog with Gulden's mustard at the ballpark would be their only meal of the day. *Author's collection.*

scorecards at the venue himself, loudly informing patrons that it was "impossible to know the players without them." Thus, "Scorecard Harry" was born. His scorecard empire soon extended to Toledo, Milwaukee, Pittsburgh, Cleveland and Washington. Stevens added Boston's Fenway Park in 1891 and the Polo Grounds in New York City in 1894. The Polo Grounds franchise included the entirety of its concession franchises, which by 1906 included the hot dog. Over time, Stevens built a concessionary empire at all the major stadiums and racetracks in the United States, from Saratoga Springs and Hialeah, Florida, to New York's Madison Square Garden to San Francisco's Candlestick Park.

Stevens's impact on ballpark menus was profound. "When I first got the concessions in New York," Stevens remembered, "no one ever heard of ice cream cones or hot dogs. Soft drinks were considered effeminate. We used to sell beer in the bleachers." Harry credited his son Frank with the idea of selling frankfurters. Soon, "Get your red hots" became the staple bellow of sale at stadiums everywhere. Stevens sold only Stahl Meyer hot dogs and the previously unknown Gulden's brown mustard. He personally designed a special metal container immersed in hot water to keep the boiled hot dogs warm. Stevens also popularized the use of a straw to allow fans to watch the game while drinking their soda.

Harry M. Stevens died on May 3, 1934. He was perhaps best known by his contemporaries for his fastidiously upright and honest business dealings. Bob Quinn, the owner of the cash-strapped Boston Braves, once offered Stevens a piece of the franchise for $25,000 cash. Stevens generously gave the money to Quinn as a loan. When the grateful owner offered to sign a promissory note, Stevens demurred, saying, "Your word is good enough for me." His epitaph should read, "He walked tall among tall people."

JOE "IRON MAN" MCGINNITY

The summaries of newspaper and magazine articles in these pages date from the early twentieth century and show that the Mahoning Valley has always taken the sport of baseball seriously. Very seriously.

The first article describes the dilemma of Charlie Crowe, the manager of the Niles, Ohio ball club. Faced with a near impossible situation, Crowe took the "red eye" train to New York City to call on fellow townsman Harry M. Stevens to utilize the latter's money and influence as the official confectioner at the Polo Grounds to "even the field" and defend the greater honor of both men's adopted hometown against the despicable shenanigans of archrival Youngstown. With Stevens's help, Crowe's desperate gamble paid off handsomely. The Niles skipper soon found his "ace in the hole" for the postseason championship series, underhand, submarine-style New York Giants pitcher "Iron Man" Joe McGinnity.

The "Iron Man" had earned his

Legendary National Hall of Fame "submarine" pitcher "Iron Man" Joe McGinnity (1871–1929). In the immediate aftermath of his Game Three "underhanded" triumph over archrival Youngstown Ohio Works, the perspiration from the heightened tension of the contest caused the pitcher's T-shirt to meld to his body like a second skin. The garment had to be sliced with scissors and peeled away. *Author's collection.*

enviable sobriquet during the 1903 season. That year, McGinnity won thirty-one games and set all-time, modern-day season records for games started and innings pitched. In just one month, August 1903, McGinnity worked one hundred innings while pitching and winning both games of a doubleheader three times within the thirty-day span. Born on March 20, 1871, in a farmhouse in Cornwall Township, Henry County, Illinois, Joe McGinnity was the third of seven children. The youngster later found work with the Decatur, Illinois Coal Company at the tender age of eight after the premature death of his father in a horrific industrial accident. But baseball was in his blood, and McGinnity spent all of his boyhood leisure time learning to control the twists and curves of his throws. A contemporary Decatur resident remembered McGinnity's frequent last-minute arrivals at the East Side ballpark, dressed in his nondescript uniform in his teen years: "Fresh from the coal mine and so hurriedly washed that much of the coal smudge still clung to the angles of his countenance. But even in those amateur days, his appearance almost invariably spelled victory for his team."

Delos Daniel "Del" Drake (1886–1965), circa 1905. The younger Drake grew up with the sport and began playing organized baseball at the age of fifteen. He signed with the Detroit Tigers in 1911, joining the legendary Ty Cobb and Sam Crawford in one of MLB's all-time best outfields. That year, Drake batted .279 with twenty stolen bases and thirty-six RBIs. Drake later starred for two seasons on the St. Louis Terriers in the Federal League. *Photo and captions by Thomas Drake.*

In the aftermath of his three-game appearance for the Niles Crowites, McGinnity continued his ten-year big-league career, finishing with 246 victories. The Iron Man averaged more wins per season than any other pitcher in MLB history, eventually earning a ticket to Cooperstown. At the conclusion of his major league career, McGinnity then pitched in the minors for two more decades, retiring with 481 total victories. McGinnity died on November 14, 1929, age fifty-eight.

11

HOW JOE McGINNITY WON A PENNANT

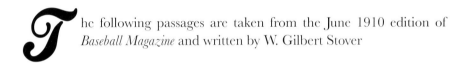

The following passages are taken from the June 1910 edition of *Baseball Magazine* and written by W. Gilbert Stover

DETERMINED TO WIN

Year after year, Warren had walloped Niles on the diamond until it became unbearable. Finally [in early 1903], a mass meeting was held; money was raised for a new ballpark and the management was turned over to Charlie Crowe, a famous pitcher. Crowe got together a fast team of the youngsters and not only defeated Warren so often it became monotonous but also every other team which they played. The Crowites were hailed as the champion independent team of Ohio.

Youngstown was the big town of the neighborhood and the location of the great Ohio Steel Works. Youngstown got jealous of the achievements of the neighboring village and near the end of the season played several games with Niles. The season ended with a tie between Niles and Youngstown.

Youngstown sportswriters claimed the championship for their team and dared Niles to play a postseason series.

The defy was accepted and a series of four games were arranged. The great Ohio Steel Works furnished the money and ex–major leaguer Marty Hogan was named as manager. While nothing was put in writing, it was agreed that both teams should use none but the players already on the roster. The first game was played in Youngstown. When the teams trotted out to practice, a gasp of astonishment and anger went up from the Niles section for it was seen that Youngstown was "loaded for bear" with an almost new lineup of Central League players. In fact, only three of the regular Youngstown players were in uniform. The Niles team struggled manfully to win but it was no use. They were up against it. Youngstown trounced Niles sharply and there was great rejoicing in the big steel city. To make matters worse, Patterson, Niles first baseman was injured, out for the season. A dark gloom settled…when the result became known, and the news spread like wildfire how Hogan had double crossed Crowe and loaded up with league players for this series. Far into the night, groups of citizens gathered and talked over the situation. Big Chief Crowe was nowhere to be seen all that night and the next day everything was just quiet as the grave around baseball headquarters. Some people thought Crowe had quit the town, others thought he was…on the hunt for players to even up with Youngstown.

Gleam in His Eye

Late that night, Crowe alighted from the train. Hundreds of people tackled him about the situation and asked what he had done and if he had any fresh players only to be met with a silent shake of the head, but there was a gleam in his eye that spelled trouble for someone and when no one was looking his face would light up with a big broad smile.

Bright and early the next morning was game day in Niles. People came in from Youngstown on every train, trolley, and every other kind of conveyance, confident in the ability of Hogan's new team to crush Niles and…back up on the betting proposition.

Lost His Smile

When Niles took the field, all at once the smile left Hogan's face, never to return for the rest of the week. Striding out to the pitcher's box in a Niles uniform was the most welcome person that appeared in Niles in many a day—none other than "Iron Man" Joe McGinnity of the New York Giants.

And how Joe did pitch that day. He was right in his glory and with that old familiar underhand ball, simply stood Youngstown's padded aggregation on the tops of its head. The Niles youngsters played like seasoned veterans behind him. He had no trouble at all in winning, the final score being three to one.

The 1903 Cleveland Indians team photo featured several players with ties to the Mahoning Valley: Hall of Famer Napoleon Lajoie (*inset, center right*), catcher Harry Bemis (*second row bottom, far right*), pitcher Earl Moore (*bottom row, second from left*) and Youngstown Giants outfielder and future Hall of Famer Elmer Flick (*bottom row, center*). *Cleveland Press Collection.*

THE LONGEST HOME RUN IN BASEBALL HISTORY

*Ha-ha. [pause]....And now at this time...I am observing [John]
Glenn's fireflies. Drifting away from me. I can observe them.*
—Gordon Cooper's Space "Diary," May 15, 1963

The following tale is included as a hazy remembrance of a conversation
between a ten-year-old fill-in paper carrier for the merchants of
downtown Niles, Ohio, and a down-on-his-luck millworker living the
end of his days at the Antler Hotel in downtown Niles.

By all accounts, it was the longest home run anyone had ever seen.
The blast once and forever broke up what had been, pitch for pitch, to
that point one of the greatest, most breathtaking postseason pitching
duels in the history of organized baseball. The date was October 2,
1903. A spillover crowd had assembled to watch game three of the
series between the visiting powerhouse Ohio Works of Youngstown
and the underdog Niles Crowites home team. The venue, constructed
on a fallow field that buttressed Main and Federal Streets, could not
accommodate the entirety of the crowd. There were as many fans
crammed outside the grounds as within. A few of the more agile cranks
perched nimbly atop the outfield fencing to watch the proceedings.
One of these was famed entertainer, songwriter and vaudeville minstrel
performer George "Honeyboy" Evans, who had a gig in Youngstown
that same evening and was able to arrive in Niles just in time. From
his unique vantage point, he would have "crow's nest" vision for any
baseball that might exit the ballpark.

Each team had notched a victory in the series, and the fierce pride
of the residents of each town made them preemptively empty their
pocketbooks to cull together this clash of two pitching titans on this
unfamiliar and decidedly proletarian turf in Niles for game three
between two righthanders, submarine hurler "Iron Man" Joe McGinnity
of the New York Giants, age thirty-two, pitching for the outlaw
Niles Crowites, and twenty-five-year-old Earl "Crossfire" Moore of
the Cleveland Indians, throwing his unhittable sidearm fireballs for
Youngstown's Ohio Works club. The roster for both teams had grown to
epic proportions, with an all-star cast of characters. The deep-pocketed
Ohio Works fielded nearly the entire roster of the MLB St. Louis Browns

in addition to Moore and his favorite receiver, Tribe catcher Harry Bemis. Increasingly, tension mounted with each pitch in this contest, heralded by contemporary sportswriters as nothing less than the 1903 Junior World Championship.

Six feet tall, handsome and square-jawed, Cleveland's Earl Moore had broken into the bigs with a bang, pitching what was then considered the first American League no-hitter on May 9, 1901, his puzzling sidearm delivery baffling the pennant-winning Chicago White Sox for nine complete innings. It was his fourth MLB start. The *Cleveland Plain Dealer* opined that Moore "showed wonderful speed—almost up to the quality possessed by Cy Young." In 1903, Moore had won nineteen games and led the American League in ERA (1.77) and fewest hits per nine innings (7.13). The Iron Man, meanwhile, was even better, leading the National League that year in wins (thirty-five), ERA (1.61), innings (408), games (fifty-one), winning percentage (.814) and even saves (five).

In this game, Niles scored two runs in the fourth inning, and the deficit, if anything, made Moore bear down even harder for the Ohio Works. The vast crowd sat hushed, mesmerized as the goose eggs collected frame by frame until the seventh inning when, with two down and nobody aboard, Niles catcher Frank Pieper turned Moore's otherwise perfect strike into a towering shot. The crowd rose to their feet and found their collective voice as the ball arced upward, higher and farther, beyond the outfield fence, beyond the shallow waters of the nearby Mosquito Creek; higher and ever farther, caught by the wind, or perhaps an unseen hand, traveling ever upward, beyond the row of tenement houses along Vienna Avenue, the ball still rising when it disappeared from view, lost finally in the bright glare of the afternoon sun. Neither team was able to score again, and so it was that Niles stunningly took a hard-fought, 3–0 victory. George "Honeyboy" Evans, meanwhile, perched precariously on the fence surrounding the grounds, had perhaps the best view of the orbit of the ball as it departed the field of play. Evans died on March 5, 1915, age forty-five. He maintained to his dying day that the ball continued its orbit heavenward unabated. His observation was put to the test in the days following Pieper's blast, as scores of Niles youths searched in vain for the prized memento.

No trace of Pieper's monumental blast was ever found.

Back with Money

It was Youngstown's turn to eat "Crowe" and how they did hate it. The Niles fans went up to the seventh heaven of delight and everybody prepared to take in the game the next day. To the surprise of everybody, early next day a bunch of "sports" from Youngstown struck town with all kinds of money to bet on the game in spite of the defeat the day before. It did not go begging either and before noon it was estimated that $10,000 had been wagered on the result and between that time and the next game $5,000 more was placed [the equivalent of $471,450 in today's dollars]. However, before the Niles people would bet, a committee had waited on McGinnity and asked him if he thought he could stand it to pitch again that day. Joe only smiled and said, "Sure I'll pitch, and I'll shut them out too."

Had Something

The stores were locked up that day, some of the mills shut down and even the Chinese laundries closed shop. Everybody headed for the ball grounds for it was felt that something was doing. Youngstown would never bet that way unless there was something up and when Youngstown took the field that "something" developed. Marty Hogan had slipped up to Cleveland and secured big Earl Moore of the Cleveland American League to pitch and Harry Bemis of the same team to catch. He had also burned the wires to Saint Louis to his old friend Jimmy McAleer for help. Friel was the shortstop and Charlie Hemphill in the outfield. Havel played third base, Freddie Mac played second, Charlie Starr played first base, Maloney center, Curley Blount rightfield. Billy Evans and Jack O'Toole umpired.

McGinnity Won

It was the old battle between the National and American League over again and the National League came out ahead [despite] the fact that Hogan had secured almost the pick of the American League. Joe McGinnity made good his boast and shut out Youngstown. He never pitched better ball than he did that bright October day. To his credit, "Doggie" Ortlieb caught McGinnity's benders in great shape and the Niles team played bang up ball.

The 1903 St. Louis Browns played two games against the Niles, Ohio Crowites. Both games were losses. Former Spiders Hall of Famer and Bonesetter Reese patient Bobby Wallace is second from left in the rear. *Author's collection.*

Youngstown could do nothing with the "Iron Man's" twisters and the game ended Niles 3 Youngstown 0.

WON THE LAST

The last game of this great series was played on Saturday in Youngstown before the biggest crowd that had ever attended a ball game in that city. Half of Niles was in attendance. It was estimated that fully 12,000 people crowded into the park while many thousands were perched on trees, houses, and fences. Crowe in the meantime, had secured Warrenite Red Ames also of the New York Giants to pitch the game, and like his partner, pitched great ball, having Youngstown guessing all the time. McGinnity captained the team and played right field and his batting and coaching played the prominent part in the victory.

Pitcher Leon "Red" Ames (1882–1936) threw right and was a switch-hitting batter. Ames played seventeen seasons and pitched in three World Series. He won the final game for Niles in the 1903 Junior League World Series. *Library of Congress.*

Although Leon Ames won 187 MLB games in his career, he was infamously known as a hard-luck pitcher, often losing games he had pitched well enough to win. On April 15, 1909, Ames pitched a nine-inning Opening Day no-hitter, only to lose the game in extra innings. *Author's collection.*

The 1905 edition of the Niles Crowites, featuring future mayor Charlie Crowe. Crowe (*center*) served as the mayor of Niles from 1916 to 1924. Future MLB great Delos Drake is pictured in the top row, third from right. His Niles teammate is Heinie Maag (*far right*), not William Maag of the *Vindicator* newspaper (who was roughly the same age). *Author's collection.*

POSTSCRIPT

For thirty-four and a half hours on May 15–16, 1963, NASA astronaut Leroy Gordon Cooper piloted his *Mercury Faith 7* capsule for a then record twenty-two orbits around the earth. On the first pass, as he neared the arc of the Betelgeuse star in the constellation Orion, with the sun rising behind him, Cooper confirmed with some glee, witnessing a mysterious patch of particles "white very whitish with almost a green like real fireflies" dancing freely in space near his capsule. The strange phenomenon had been first observed some months earlier by Ohio-born astronaut John Glenn. The presence of "fireflies" in outer space remained an inexplicable mystery for all except a small group of septuagenarians living in an obscure corner of the universe called Niles, Ohio, in the Mahoning Valley. For them, the long-sought mystery had been solved at last. Frank Pieper's home run ball, transmogrified into elemental particles, had been twice discovered, still sailing upward toward heaven itself.*

---

* Hard-luck Earl Moore lost his 1901 no-hitter and the game in the tenth inning. His teammates were unable to give the hurler any offensive support. In 2000, MLB baseball excised any no-hitter that extended beyond nine innings. Moore's no-hitter exists no more in the record books. The decision also excised perhaps the greatest pitching performance in baseball history, when Pittsburgh Pirates right-hander Harvey Haddix pitched a nine-inning perfect game on May 26, 1959, but lost in extra innings.

Moore's promising MLB career was derailed by a drive through the box in 1905 that tore apart his left foot so badly that he won just six games in the next three seasons. The pitcher would come back for the Philadelphia Phillies after a stint in the minors, winning eighteen games in 1909 and twenty-two games in 1910.

Gordon Cooper claimed to have seen dozens of circular-shaped UFOs during his many years as a pilot. He discussed their sighting(s) in a televised interview with Merv Griffin.

12

BILLY EVANS AND THE "GREATEST PITCHER THE WORLD HAS EVER KNOWN"

Baseball and Billy Evans were and are synonymous. The sport never had a better booster. He wrote it, umpired it, and administered it. Most important, he loved the game and sold it everywhere he went.
—*Ed Bang,* Cleveland News *newspaper, 1954*

William George Evans was born in Chicago on February 10, 1884. Shortly after, his family moved to Youngstown for the work in the Carnegie steel mills. Evans attended city schools and graduated from Rayen High School in 1901. He enrolled at Cornell University and played varsity baseball under fellow Hall of Famer Hughie Jennings until his father's premature death forced Evans's return to the Valley to help support the family. Evans subsequently took a job with the *Youngstown Vindicator* newspaper. He was covering a minor-league game when the scheduled umpire was a no-show. Evans was desperately enlisted as a fill-in for $15, equivalent to an entire week's salary at the newspaper. His officiating was so spot-on that Evans was offered a permanent position at $150 per month. He was later hired as a major league umpire in 1905 on Valley resident Jimmy McAleer's endorsement to American League president Ban Johnson after a controversial but correct call at home plate during an Ohio Pennsylvania League game in Niles. Evans became, at twenty-two, the youngest arbiter in Major League history and was forever known as the "Boy Umpire." In a twenty-plus-year career, Evans umpired 3,319 MLB games, including calling balls and strikes as the home plate umpire for 1,717 contests. Evans also worked six World Series starting in 1919. Throughout his lengthy career, Evans wrote a syndicated sports column for the Newspaper Enterprise Association.

Following the 1927 season, Billy Evans retired from umpiring to become the first "official" general manager in MLB history, working for the Cleveland Indians. He was hired for that position by a consortium of new Tribe owners, including team president Alva Bradley. Two of the greatest Cooperstown Hall of Fame players in Cleveland baseball history were "inked" under his watch, including center fielder Earl Averill, whom he scouted and personally signed. The signing of right-handed fireball pitcher extraordinaire Bob Feller also happened under his watch. In his first-person account to Tribe owner Alva Bradley and Billy Evans, veteran Indians bird dog Cy "C.C." Slapnicka flatly declared that sixteen-year-old Bob Feller would be the "greatest pitcher the world had ever known."

Earl Averill was the career home run leader for the Indians/Guardians with 226 dingers until fellow Hall of Famer Jim Thome shattered the mark with 337. As a Tribesman, Averill was named to the All-Star team consecutively from 1933 to 1938. Averill's line drive to the foot of Dizzy Dean in the 1938 All-Star Game essentially ended the career of the Hall of Fame pitcher.

Billy Evans, meanwhile, following his stint as the Tribe general manager, worked for the Boston Red Sox, the Detroit Tigers and the Cleveland Rams of the National Football League. He also served as president of the minor league Southern Association from 1942 to 1946. Evans died after suffering a stroke on February 15, 1954. The former umpire was seventy-eight years old.

THE FOLLOWING SYNDICATED OP-ED appeared in newspapers across the country on September 25, 1930, shortly before the deaths of both Charlie Crowe and Jimmy McAleer. Charles Henry Crowe, the four-time Niles mayor, died at the Cleveland Clinic on February 7, 1931, age fifty-nine. James Robert McAleer, suffering the painful ravages of inoperable cancer, despondent over a recent divorce and still unmoved by the betrayal of former ally Ban Johnson, shot himself at his Youngstown, Ohio Park Avenue home on April 28, 1931, and died the following day. He was sixty-six.

SEEING BIG LEAGUE BASEBALL

By Billy Evans, sportswriter, big league umpire and general manager of the Cleveland Indians

1930 Bell Syndicate

The game that was responsible for my big-league career comes back as clearly as though it was played yesterday instead of more than 20 years ago. It was between Niles and Youngstown, two great rivals in those days. Going into the last half of the ninth inning, Niles was trailing Youngstown by one run. I believe the score was seven to six.

Now all unknown to me there was sitting in the stands that day a man whose presence was to alter my whole career. His name was James McAleer, the famous Jimmy McAleer, at that time manager of the St. Louis Browns in the American League.

St. Louis it seems was playing at Cleveland and McAleer had run down to Niles to get a line on a player on the Youngstown club, Charlie Starr by name. So, there in the grandstand sat McAleer....And neither he nor I imagined for a moment that he was to do a little umpire scouting for the American League on the side.

That game was one of those close, hotly fought contests we umpires know as "tough ones." Niles made a great rally in the ninth and filled the bases with two outs. A hit would bring in two runs and win the old ball game.

Jimmy McAleer was the 1903 manager of the St. Louis Browns as well as the "discoverer" of Billy Evans, the "Boy Umpire." McAleer recommended Evans to American League president Ban Johnson in the aftermath of a correct but questionable call in a Niles, Ohio minor-league game against archrivals Ohio Works of Youngstown. *Library of Congress.*

A base on balls would tie the score, and the batter, Billy Thomas, worked Stewart, the Youngstown pitcher, to a two and three count.

"Bust it out!" shouted the Niles fans. "Bust it out, Billy, or wait it out. A walk's as good as a hit. Make him put it over."

And then Stewart wound up and pitched. Thomas saw the ball coming and let it go by. In fact, he even fell down as if in the act of avoiding being hit. And then he started to trot to first base and the fans had visions of a tie score.

But I had my eye on that ball too. It was a fast-breaking curve, and it took a lot of nerve to throw a pitch in a pinch like that. It was a wide curve that had cut the corner of the plate. Upward I jerked my thumb.

"Strike three." I bellowed. And then things happened.

Those fans, seeing Thomas fall to the ground, by pantomime had taken it for granted that the last pitch had been a ball. When I called him out, they believed I was committing robbery and throwing the game to Youngstown.

The "Boy Umpire" Billy Evans (1884–1956) had a varied career in professional baseball. He received his start in the Mahoning Valley as an umpire for the minor league Ohio Pennsylvania League and moonlighted as a sportswriter for the Youngstown *Vindicator*. In addition to his Hall of Fame career as an arbiter, he also wrote a widely syndicated sports column and was the first to hold the "official" designation of general manager of a ball club. Pitcher Bob Feller was signed on his watch. *Library of Congress*.

They poured out of their seats and made straight for the plate where I was still standing. They threatened me, called me every name under the sun, they jostled me, pulled at my clothes, and probably would have mobbed me right there if it hadn't been for Charlie Crowe, pitcher, and manager of the Niles team. If anybody on that ballfield had the right to protest my decision it was Charlie Crowe. But being fair minded and realizing my peril, he came to my side to help me.

"I'm not kicking Billy," he told me as he stood beside me to face the throng of fans, "You called it as you saw it and I'm satisfied, and I'm going to see that you get back safely to your hotel." I'll never forget that walk back to the little hotel as long as I live. In reality, it was but a few short blocks but to me it seemed as long as a marathon race. The mob followed at my heels.

And all that time, I was marching straight towards the big leagues, and I didn't know it.

"The Greatest Pitcher the World Has Ever Known."

Only God can give a man a fastball.
—Wilbert Robinson

I was a bonus baby. I got two autographed baseballs,
and a scorecard from the 1935 All Star game.
—Bob Feller

Hour after hour, the staccato cacophony continued as fastballs pounded into the rented pillows at the New Orleans hotel, spring training headquarters for the Cleveland Indians baseball team. Across the room, teen pitching impresario Bob Feller, burning with unquenchable flame and fire, honed the mechanics of his gifted right arm, transforming the Louisiana hotel room from a place of rest into an impromptu training facility. Roommate Roy Hughes watched and remembered: "You couldn't go to sleep, listening to that Plop! Plop! All night." For the serious-minded Feller, the sun-drenched workouts at New Orleans' Heinemann Park served as a mere prelude for the real labor to come.

Robert William Andrew Feller arrived at the major leagues fully formed, the kilowatt bioluminescence of his star power manifest in the eye-popping, nearly impossible velocity of his fastball. Indeed, his explosive fireball ranked with the absolute best. He once threw "unofficially" the fastest pitch ever recorded with a speed device, 107.9 miles per hour. The Indians phenom struck out fifteen batters in his first start. Three weeks later, the teenager fanned seventeen, matching his age, to establish the major league record. Fellow's rookie season of 1936 ended before his senior year of high school. In the span of a few short weeks, Feller had compiled a 5-3 record with one save. He struck out seventy-six batters in sixty-two innings and posted a team-best 3.34 ERA. In his wake, sportswriters struggled for superlatives while long-suffering Cleveland Indian fans savored the team's suddenly bright prospects.

Bob Feller was born on November 3, 1918, in Van Meter, Iowa, a proletarian farm community, population three hundred, not far from the capital of Des Moines. William Feller, a former sandlot player, recognized his son's incredible athletic skill while the boy was still a toddler and began grooming his eager prodigy for the major leagues, first with father-son games of catch. Their workouts, which began after farm chores, intensified with each passing year. In 1924, William installed a Delco battery to power the barnyard beyond sunset and later changed their cash crop from corn to wheat to allow more practice during the harvest season. The Fellers switched to the Methodist faith when their Catholic priest criticized baseball played on the Sabbath. Family outings to Des Moines coincided with the game schedules of the House of David and the Kansas City Monarchs. And as the boy grew, so did his talent. At nine, the youngster could throw a baseball 275 feet. Four years later, the Fellers collaborated to build Oakview Park, a field constructed from acreage cleared from the family homestead. It was a visionary project, transforming roughhewn pasture into a viable ballfield, complete with bleachers, an outfield fence and a working scoreboard. The Fellers formed a team, the Oakviews, provided uniforms and "scheduled games throughout the summer." On most Sundays, two or three hundred fans paid twenty-five Depression-era cents to watch the thirteen-year-old rising star strike out traveling teams from Des Moines and elsewhere in an area stretching as far as Omaha, Nebraska. The Oakview enterprise generated enough revenue to sustain itself and was the culmination of the Fellers' shared aspirations, as father bequeathed to son "a real-life Field of Dreams more than 50 years before the movie."

In addition to the Oakviews, Feller pitched for his school, Van Meter Consolidated; the American Legion traveling squad, located in nearby Adel, Iowa; and, for thirty dollars a game, the Farmers Union club in the Iowa chapter of the American Amateur Baseball Congress (AABC). In his sophomore year of high school, Feller pitched five no-hitters, adding a sixth in his debut with the adult Farmers Union team, striking out twenty-two opposing batters. In his next start, the youngster pitched a 1-0 shutout, notching nineteen Ks on the scoreboard. With Feller as their star, the Farmers Union team went on to win the Iowa State amateur baseball championship. Feller posted a 25-4 record that year, averaging 19.4 strikeouts per game. With a blistering fastball that rose and danced at the plate, Feller found that he could strike out almost anyone at any age. His delivery ranged from overhand, three-fourths and sidearm, delivering fastballs and curves at any angle with equal devastation.

Only the vagaries of genetics can manufacture a fastball, and the teen's lineage was splendorous. William Feller was a former sandlot player, and Bob's maternal grandfather, Edward Forrett, was rumored to have been the "best-durned pitcher in IoWAY." It was perhaps such folk tales of undiscovered talent that inspired Indians bird dog Cy Slapnicka to create an impressive scouting combine in his native Hawkeye State. As the testimonials flooded the Indians' grapevine from awestruck umpires in the Iowa amateur league, Slapnicka decided to visit the Feller family farm during a scouting trip initiated for another promising prospect, Clyde Passeau. Their initial meeting proved to be the stuff of legend: Feller and father were working in the field when the tall, bespectacled Slapnicka winnowed his way through the field of wheat, coat draped over his arm in the sweltering heat. By all accounts, it was an awkward affair, merely establishing young Feller's next scheduled pitching assignment in Des Moines two days later. For his part, Slapnicka was impressed by the teen's chiseled physique, steeled by the industry of hard farm labor. But nothing could prepare the Slapnicka for the display of power that he saw from Feller on the mound. After watching the first pitch or two, Slapnicka positioned himself out of the pitcher's line of vision behind the backstop, where he sat transfixed on the bumper of a parked car. At that moment, Slapnicka realized the "dream of every baseball scout who ever had a flat tire on a country road, the definitive dream"—he had discovered the greatest pitching talent in Cleveland Indians history.

Forgetting Passeau, Slapnicka revisited the Feller family farm later that evening, armed with stationary purloined from the Des Moines hotel, several trinkets of Indians memorabilia and a one-dollar bill. Slapnicka penned a crude, 134-word document signing young Feller to the Class D Fargo Moorhead Twins baseball club for the 1936 season, the lowest rung of the Indians organization. Returning to Cleveland immediately after Feller signed, Slapnicka met with Cleveland Indians president Alva Bradley and

Tribe pitcher Bob Feller (1918–2010) and catcher Rollie Hemsley (1907–1972) collaborated on the April 16, 1940 Opening Day 1–0 no-hitter at Chicago's Comiskey Park. Hemsley was an early success story of the Alcoholics Anonymous group. *Author's collection.*

general manager Billy Evans in a closed-door session and gave the following assessment: "I suppose this seems like the same old stuff to you, but I want you to believe me. This boy I found out in Iowa will be the greatest pitcher the world has ever seen. His fastball is fast and fuzzy, never goes in a straight line, it wiggles and shoots around."

Over time, Slapnicka's heated hyperbole proved accurate. In a seventeen-year career, Bob Feller became the winningest pitcher in Cleveland Indians history, pitching 570 games, 44 shutouts and 2,581 strikeouts in 3,827 innings while winning 20 or more games six times, firing 3 no-hitters and hurling 12 one-hitters. Feller set a single-game strikeout record of 18 on October 2, 1938, and a season strikeout record of 348 in 1946. (Both records have since been broken.) Feller retired with 266 victories and was elected to the Baseball Hall of Fame in 1962, his first year of eligibility. His uniform number 19 has been retired by the Indians/Guardians. His accomplishments are even more amazing given the fact that he gave up his prime years in service to his country. Two days after the Japanese bombed Pearl Harbor, Feller enlisted in the navy and spent the prime of his career aboard the USS *Alabama*, where he earned eight battle stars. There will always be conjecture and speculation as to how many more victories the fastballer would have achieved but for his forty-four months of service in World War II.

One record that remains intact is Feller's fantastic Opening Day no-hitter in Chicago on April 12, 1940, with Rollie Hemsley catching. In that game, Feller threw nothing but fastballs after the second inning due to the vagaries of the strong wind that day at Comiskey Park.*

---

* It must be something in the water. Another Valley great, Warren, Ohio hurler Leon "Red" Ames (who won the fourth game of the famous Niles Youngstown series in 1903) pitched a nine-inning no-hitter on Opening Day, April 15, 1909, for the New York Giants against the Brooklyn Superbas (Dodgers) but lost the no-hitter in the tenth inning on Whitey Alperman's one-out double. Ames later lost the game in the thirteenth inning. The Giants were unable to mount any offense in the first nine frames, as Brooklyn's Kaiser Wilhelm pitched a one-hitter.

NAPOLEON LAJOIE, ELMER FLICK, TERRY TURNER, JOHN SCHEIBLE AND THE GREATEST PENNANT RACE IN CLEVELAND HISTORY

[Napoleon Lajoie] may not be the sun in the baseball firmament,
but he is a bright, particular star.
—*Pennsylvania Supreme Court*

*A*mid the haze of tobacco smoke and the festive air of glasses held high in the gathering places of the sporting gentry of the Mahoning Valley and elsewhere, there was much cause for celebration: Napoleon Lajoie had been signed by the major-league Cleveland Blues. It was June 3, 1902. Though rain had delayed the second baseman's appearance until the morrow, the spectacular news brought instant excitement to fans and ended long weeks of rumors and speculation regarding the most famous player in baseball. The year before, while playing for the Philadelphia Athletics, this Bonaparte had conquered the sporting world with a batting average of .426 in the new American League. A line-drive hitter of incredible power, the lissome right-hander was the first player to bat above .400 throughout an entire season. Lajoie won the batting Triple Crown by the largest margin in baseball history. He also led the new loop in virtually every fielding category. Ragtime scriveners crowned him "King Larry." Lajoie's effortless dominance on the field made him seem at times more a creature of myth than of substance, his bat supplanting the fabled axe of Paul Bunyan. And in the passage of a century and more, no single individual has had such a profound impact on the history of the Cleveland Indians. And so, the merriment and the ale flowed freely through the night.

When Lajoie's signing was announced, the club box office was besieged; thousands of tickets were sold within hours. The following day, a huge weekday crowd of nearly ten thousand fans crammed into League Park. Lajoie performed every bit to expectations, hitting one of his trademark doubles and later scoring. The slick-fielding second baseman also figured in two rally-killing double plays. Lajoie then went on a tear, batting .451 through early July. He also treated fans to the first grand slam in franchise history. Lajoie's quiet leadership had instantly transformed the Cleveland nine into legitimate pennant contenders.

Lajoie (pronounced "Lads-aWAY") was every inch a picture player, larger than life, comfortable in the glare of the spotlight. With his cap turned rakishly to the side and his upturned collar, the affable Frenchman personified a masculine and sublimely quixotic mixture of grace and finesse with raw power, quickly becoming the darling of fans. Born in Woonsocket, Rhode Island, on September 5, 1874, Lajoie's first professional baseball contract was with Fall River in 1896, on a hastily handwritten document on the reverse side of an envelope. Lajoie reached the majors later that year. The second baseman remains forever linked to the Mahoning Valley when his career was extended by the tactile machinations of "Bonesetter" Reese.

IN THE INAUGURAL 1901 season, the Cleveland Bluebirds under manager Jimmy McAleer finished seventh in the fledgling American League, sporting only three up-and-coming players: third baseman Bill Bradley; pitcher Earl Moore; and aging Mahoning Valley great, catcher Bob Wood, who hailed from Youngstown, Ohio. Wood had played on the Findlay, Ohio mixed-race teams of Bud Fowler and Grant Johnson, sponsored by William Drake. Drake was born in Girard, Ohio, and was also on the roster of the famed 1883 Grays/NYPANOs team. Apart from those three, Cleveland fans remained unimpressed, and the Bluebirds posted the lowest attendance figures in the league. It was rumored that their continued weakness at the box office would cause the troubled franchise to be relocated to Pittsburgh or Cincinnati. The prospects for the future were dismal. Indeed, five previous franchises had failed. It was "King Larry's" mere presence and drawing power that utterly transformed the franchise that would later bear his name.

In 1902, the Cleveland franchise (renamed the Bronchos) was also strengthened with the addition of hard-hitting outfielder and future Hall of Famer Elmer Flick. Born in Bedford, Ohio, on January 11, 1876, Flick began his baseball career with the Youngstown Puddlers of the Interstate League in 1896. Puddlers player-manager John Scheible, himself a former major leaguer, took a chance on the slightly built twenty-year-old for the position of left field, sight unseen. Formerly a catcher, Flick hastily prepared for his "garden" trial through an exercise regimen of running and playing catch by bouncing a baseball off the side of a building. On a lathe, Flick also turned his own bat, which served him well at the plate. In just thirty-one games, Flick collected fifty-seven hits, batted .431 and recorded five doubles, nine triples and six home runs. His defense at the new position was another matter, with an atrocious .826 fielding average. In a January 1963 interview for the *Cleveland Record*, Flick recalled that Scheible told him that, as an outfielder, "I wasn't so hot.... 'But you can sure sting that ball.'"

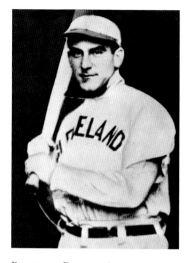

Bonesetter Reese patient and Cleveland player-manager Napoleon "Larry" Lajoie was the sixth player inducted into baseball's Hall of Fame. Lajoie is widely considered to be Cleveland's all-time best second baseman. He was so dominant that the team during his tenure was officially renamed the Naps in his honor. *Cleveland Public Library*.

Flick subsequently signed with Dayton in the Interstate League in 1897, recorded 183 hits in 126 games, led the league with twenty triples, batted .386, stole twenty-five bases and quickly became a favorite of fans, who chanted a ditty in homage to their diminutive star: "Elmer Flick you are slick / Hit a homer pretty quick." The outfielder even improved his fielding average to .921. Not surprisingly, given Flick's otherworldly performance in the minors, he was fast-tracked into the major leagues, signing with guru manager George Stallings of the Philadelphia Phillies for the 1898 season.

SOUTHPAW HURLER JOHN G. Scheible was born in Youngstown on February 16, 1866. He debuted impressively for minor league Youngstown in the Tri-State League in 1890 and later passed through several independent teams in Ohio and Illinois. In 1893, he starred with Altoona in the Pennsylvania State League when the Cleveland Spiders signed him during the final month of the season. In his first MLB start on September 8, 1893,

Scheible became the first major-leaguer to debut with a shutout at the new sixty-foot, six-inch distance when he beat the Washington Senators under Al Maul, 7–0. In a remembrance years later, *The Sporting News* reported that Scheible was pounded hard that day, but every drive was hit right at someone. Scheible's luck (if it was that) ran out in his next start a week later, as he lost to the Baltimore Orioles, 9–2, and was unceremoniously cut from the team shortly after.

The year following, Scheible returned to the minors and culled together a snazzy 16-2 record, with both losses coming in the ninth inning. His near-perfect performance earned him a return to the majors with the Philadelphia Phillies. On September 20, 1894, against Cap Anson's Chicago Cubs, Scheible lasted just a third of an inning as ten runs crossed the plate. He was removed in favor of Monkey Johnson in what would prove to be a 20–4 Phillies loss. Later that evening, at the Tremont House, Scheible fell in the bathtub and accidently severed a tendon in his left leg, bleeding for three hours before summoning assistance. Despite the injury, he returned to the minors with a bang at Bridgetown in the Southern New Jersey League, earning him yet another invite to the Cleveland Spiders for the 1896 season. He became instead the player-manager for his hometown Youngstown Puddlers and had them winning, coaxing the maximum performance from his players while taking an occasional trip to the pitcher's box. Due to his success, Scheible returned to manage Youngstown for the 1897 season but could no longer pitch and was released in a July austerity move, just one month before his August 20, 1897 death from typhoid fever. He was thirty-one. Meanwhile, with Flick, Lajoie and sophomore Hall of Fame pitcher Addie Joss, known as the "Twirlologist," along with future Youngstown hurler Earl Moore and catchers Harry Bemis and Nig Clarke, Cleveland was favored to win the 1903 American League pennant. All players except Joss and Clarke had ties to the Mahoning Valley: Flick first played professional baseball in Youngstown with the Puddlers, Moore and Bemis played for Youngstown in the 1903 Junior World Series against Niles and Lajoie and Terry Turner had their careers extended by the redoubtable Bonesetter Reese. Cleveland finished third as Lajoie led all batters in hitting and slugging. That year, a newspaper contest was held to rename the ball club. The overwhelming favorite was the Napoleons, or Naps, a tribute to their star. The moniker would stick for Lajoie's long tenure with the club.

Cleveland improved its roster with the late-season acquisition of yet another player with ties to the Valley, shortstop Terry Turner. Born on February 28, 1881, in Sandy Lake Pennsylvania, Terrence Lamont Turner was the quintessential utility player, possessing great glove skills and mastery of the "inside game," willing to sacrifice his own batting average to advance base runners. "Inside work does not permit individual playing as much as where every man is a unit, but it brings results,"

With one of the all-time great glove men playing next to him, Lajoie improved his numbers in 1904, once again leading in batting and slugging (.381 and .554, respectively). He also led the circuit in hits (211), doubles (50) and RBIs (102). His namesake Naps fell to fourth place, however. Cleveland's brass decided that Lajoic should also manage the club. In 1905, his first year at the helm, the Naps were winning in the early going and were six games in front when a spiking felled the star, who developed blood poisoning from the dye in his socks. Lajoie's convalescence lasted for weeks. Six games ahead when the spiking occurred, the Naps fell six games behind when he returned, the team finishing a tepid fourth. The following two years were also marked by disappointment and frustration. The fans derisively nicknamed the team the "Napkins" for their penchant to "fold" in the heat of the season.

Then came 1908.

During spring training, the Detroit Tigers, who had won the AL pennant in 1907, initiated a trade offer: Ty Cobb even-up for Elmer Flick. Cobb was fighting with his teammates and causing dissension. The Naps quickly refused their offer, a decision they would soon regret. A short time later, on the trip back to Cleveland, Flick became seriously ill with a mysterious stomach ailment. The illness did not abate, effectively ending his baseball career. During the entire 1908 season, he played just three games.

More bad news happened when Terry Turner was felled by a headshot in the early season, then hurt his arm on his return. The shortstop paid a visit to Bonesetter Reese, who "cured" the injury but declared that Turner could not throw effectively for several months. A short trial proved the doctor correct. George Perring replaced Turner.

Somehow, despite the loss of two of its best players, the Naps remained in contention, in no small part thanks to the strong arms of the pitchers: team ace Addie Joss, who was having a season for the ages; Bob Rhodes, whose "Merry Widow" curve began to baffle the opposition; and Glenn Liebhardt, who won a career-high fifteen victories.

On September 9, the Naps were in fourth place, five and a half games behind the league-leading Tigers. The Chicago White Sox and the St. Louis Browns were second and third, respectively. On that date, however, Cleveland began one of the hottest winning streaks in baseball history. All of the pitchers caught fire, and the Naps acquired a failed pitcher turned outfielder from the minors, Wilbur Goode, who burned up the league when he arrived, winning a crucial road game against the Tigers with a towering home run. On September 18, Bob Rhodes curved his way to a brilliant 2–1 no-hitter against the Boson Red Sox. The Naps won twenty contests against just three defeats to close out the month.

By October 1, Cleveland was mere percentage points behind Detroit with five games to play. Mathematically, the Napoleons needed at least four victories to clinch the pennant. Pitching would be the key.

Chicago White Sox at Cleveland Napoleons, October 2, 1908

League Park hosted 10,596 fans, who elbowed their way in to see a dream pitching matchup between two future Hall of Famers: Chicago spitball artist Ed Walsh, with thirty-nine wins that year, against the Naps' "fadeaway" screwball pitcher Addie Joss, undefeated since September 5 and working with catcher Nig Clarke. The umpire was future Hall of Famer Tommy Connolly. Because of the prospect of an extra-inning game, the start time had been moved up by half an hour.

From the first pitch, it was clear that both hurlers were utterly dominating. Through the second inning, Walsh had already struck out four batters. In the third frame, Naps centerfielder Joe Birmingham slapped the first hit of the day with a buttercup thumper single to his playing turf in right-center field. Considered a master of the delayed steal, Birmingham coaxed Walsh to throw to first just as the center fielder broke for the keystone base. The hurried follow-up throw struck Birmingham on the shoulder, and the ball ricocheted into deep right field. In the confusion, Birmingham advanced to third base. Later in the inning, with two outs and two strikes on the leadoff batter, Wilbur Goode, Walsh threw a spitter that got past his battery mate Ossie Schreckengost. The errant ball roiled to the stands while Birmingham scored standing up. Wilbur Goode struck out on the next pitch, but the Naps led, 1–0.

Meanwhile, Joss's fadeaway pitch was working to perfection, as the White Sox kept pounding pitch after pitch into the dirt. Joss's pitches had always possessed devastating speed; as a youth, he once shattered a brick on his uncle's Wisconsin farm. On this day, his pitching was never finer or faster. According to contemporary reporters, the batted balls were taking some "queer hops in the infield." Lajoie's fielding was nothing short of flawless.

At one point in the fourth inning, Lajoie had retired five straight batters. Twice he had raced behind the box to make spectacular plays. As out after out were recorded, the crowd grew still. Joss had never pitched a no-hitter. Now, history loomed.

In the seventh, Sox manager Fielder Jones managed to work the "Twirlologist" to a full count. Joss threw a fastball tight into the zone. The bat never left Jones's shoulder for a called strike three. In the eighth, Joss retired the White Sox in order and had now faced the minimum twenty-four batters.

Just one inning remained.

In the finale, to break the spell, the Sox manager called on three pinch hitters. Doc White lined a daisy cutter for the first out. Joss struck out the next batter, Jiggs Donahue. Two down. Then came "Honest" John Anderson, a strong, switch-hitting Norwegian-born athlete who boxed and wrestled during the off-season. Anderson fouled the first pitch down the left-field baseline. The next pitch was a called strike two. The tension in the stands became almost unbearable. Cigars remained unlit in the anticipation. Joss threw another fastball. Anderson rapped the pitch sharply behind third baseman Bill Bradley. It was Bradley's first chance of the game, and he made a low, hurried throw to first base. George Stovall scooped up the ball just in time to retire the batter as the crowd found its voice at last. The game was over. Joss had pitched one for the record books. A perfect game. The twenty-eight-year-old had completed his masterpiece with a mere seventy-eight pitches over a span of just eighty-nine minutes. Ed Walsh had scattered just four hits and fanned fifteen Naps in defeat, including Wilbur Goode four times. But it was not enough against perfection.

Chicago White Sox at Cleveland Napoleons, Saturday, October 3

The mood was jubilant indeed as a record 20,729 fans elbowed their way into League Park for the final home game of the season. From September 9, the Napoleons had gained five full games on the leaders and was the hottest team in baseball. For this game, it was Glenn Liebhardt against Frank Smith for Chicago. Lajoie replaced the slumping Wilbur Goode with Josh Clark in the outfield, and Harry Bemis replaced Nig Clark as the catcher. Otherwise, the lineup was the same as the previous day. The Naps appeared tight before the game, and a series of miscues in the second inning put Cleveland behind early. Lajoie bobbled a throw by Bemis to set up two base runners. Later, with two outs, Liebhardt elected to pitch to Lee Tannehill instead of issuing a pass to get to the pitcher. Tannehill's daisy-cutter single to right field drove in both runners. The Browns led, 2–0. In the bottom half of the inning, Lajoie partially redeemed his earlier error by stroking a double. He later scored. But the White Sox added an insurance run in the sixth inning as Frank Isbell crossed home on Freddy Parents's double.

In the seventh frame, with the score still 3–1, reserve shortstop George Perring, using a sixty-five-year-old bat lathed from prison scaffolding, reached second on a muffled fly to Patsy Daugherty. Pinch hitter Clarke then struck out for pitcher Liebhardt. Josh Clarke, the Naps' leadoff batter, reached first on a line drive. Perring held at third. Clarke promptly stole second base, and third baseman Bill Bradley was issued a pass to load the bases. To stop the hemorrhaging, White Sox ace Ed Walsh was quickly summoned to relieve. Walsh's inside pitch to Bill Hinchman was tapped to third, resulting in a force of Perring at home. That brought Lajoie to the plate with the bases full and two outs. The admiring home crowd watched as "King" Larry drew his signature line in the dirt with the business end of the bat, stood back in the box and waited for the pitch. The season had come to this: a moment of high drama as each team featured their best player with the pennant squarely in the balance. On the first pitch, Walsh threw a spitter that broke down and inside. Lajoie fouled the pitch into the bleachers for strike one. Walsh fired another spitball on the outside. Lajoie fouled it back into the stands. Strike two. Wash then threw perhaps the finest pitch of his career, an overhand fastball that raised at the plate. Lajoie, a notorious fastball hitter, watched the throw go by without an offer. Strike three. Walsh remembered that Lajoie "sort of grinned and tossed his bat toward the bench without a word." The Cleveland threat had ended with a whimper. Walsh called the moment the high point of his baseball career. In the eighth inning, first baseman George Stovall scored a run for the Naps, but the team could do no more. The final score: White Sox 3, Naps 2. Hard luck Glenn Liebhardt was the loser. Lajoie's failure at the plate was quickly the buzz of the town, his failure comparable to the mythical strikeout in "Casey at the Bat:"

Oh, somewhere in this favored land the sun is shining bright.
The band is playing somewhere, and somewhere hearts are light,
And somewhere men are laughing and somewhere children shout;
But there is no joy in Mudville—mighty Casey has struck out.
(Ernest Thayer, San Francisco Examiner, *June 3, 1888)*

For the Naps, three games remained, all on the road against the St. Louis Browns, who were managed by Youngstowner Jimmy McAleer. The Naps needed a sweep to win the American League crown. The Browns, feeling the sting from their recent elimination, pulled out all the stops to win. Excitement was high. Ten thousand fans were on hand for this Sunday matchup: Bob Rhoades against Barney Pelty of the Browns. Umpire Jack Egan arrived late. His train had been delayed.

As the game began, Rhoades fell behind early. The Browns scored two runs in the third and added another in the fourth. Clearly not at his best, Rhoades was lifted in the fifth inning for pinch hitter Wilbur Goode. The gambit worked. Goode drew a walk and later scored. Relief pitcher Heinie Berger started the bottom half of the inning but was quickly replaced after walking the first two batters. Lajoie now had to go for broke. Addie Joss was sent to the hill. Joss had volunteered to pitch before the game got out of hand. In the box, Joss pitched masterfully in relief, completely shutting down the Browns. One batter after another fell to his drop shoots. Joss's heroic efforts on just one day's rest seemed to inspire his teammates. In the seventh inning, they rallied to tie the score, 3–3. And in the top of the ninth, with two outs and runners on the corners, Bill Hinchman lined a hard grounder up the middle to shortstop Bobby Wallace. The former Spiders star made an instinctive stab at the ball, knocking it down and firing to first base while the runner crossed home plate for the go-ahead run. Browns first baseman Tom Jones then fired the ball back to the catcher to stop a second run from scoring. The Cleveland bench became delirious for a moment.

In the confusion, umpire Eagan had signaled that Hinchman was out at first, thus ending the inning. Catcalls cascaded across the grounds, echoing disbelief at the call. The Naps rushed the umpire in protest, but Egan was adamant. Hinchman was out. He had not hustled to first, probably assuming that Wallace could not make the play. Darkness finally halted the contest in the eleventh inning with the score still tied. The fine relief effort by Joss was in vain. Worse, the Naps would be without the services of their best pitcher for the remainder of the season. Newspapers across the Lake Erie shoreline were unanimous in their assessment: umpire Egan blew the call. It was reported that the decision was made late and without emphasis. From his vantage point, the Browns' first baseman certainly believed that Hinchman was safe, necessitating the throw home. Nonetheless, the game was rescheduled as a doubleheader for the following day.

CLEVELAND NAPOLEONS AT SAINT LOUIS BROWNS, MONDAY, OCTOBER 5

On this day, 9,500 fans watched as Naps pitcher Glenn Liebhardt faced Bill Dineen for the biggest game in franchise history. Liebhardt was not sharp, giving up a run in the first inning. He seemed to settle down, and in the top of the fifth, George Stovall doubled to right field and later scored when Naps pitcher Liebhardt lined a shot into shallow center field. The score was now tied at one.

In the next inning, the Browns' leadoff batter lined a hard grounder to second base. Lajoie fielded the ball cleanly but overthrew for a two-base error. On the next play, outfielder Dode Criss lined another hard grounder to Bill Hinchman in left field. Hinchman caught the ball and fired to the cutoff man at short, George Perring, who pegged a perfect strike to Bill Bradley at third base. Bradley received the throw in time but somehow missed the tag. Both runners were declared safe on the fielder's choice. According to some, the runner was out and umpire Egan blew another call. Later in the inning, a single by Jimmy Williams score both runners. The Naps failed to mount another threat, and the game ended—St. Louis 3, Cleveland 1. For Cleveland, the pennant race was over. Returning alone to the hotel after the game, the tough-as-nails Lajoie broke down in his room. The long season had taken its toll.

Cleveland won both of the remaining games to finish the season with a record of 90-64, just .004 percentage points behind the Detroit Tigers, who capitalized on a rainout game. The early-season loss of Valley stars Elmer Flick and Terry Turner had proved to be devastating.

Lajoie was replaced as manager by Youngstown native Deacon McGuire midway through the 1909 season after a horrible start. He remained with the club as a player through the 1914 season. During that time, the Naps never meaningfully contended for the pennant.

14

GEORGE BURNS, STAN COVELESKI, GEORGE UHLE, MARTY HOGAN AND THE WORLD CHAMPION 1920 CLEVELAND INDIANS

Marty Hogan was one of the speediest sprinters that the game has ever seen…but he is dim of vision in sizing up pitchers.
—Washington Post, *April 1898*

He loved the outdoors and loved to pitch, but he sure hated to talk.
—*Bill Wambsganss on teammate Stan Coveleski*

*I*n a gala pregame ceremony at Cleveland's League Park, Niles, Ohio mayor Charles Crowe presented a "handsome" testimonial gold watch to its well-traveled native son, twenty-seven-year-old Cleveland Indians first baseman George Henry Burns, the sporting world's hero of the moment in the 1920 World Series. Following a brief dugout ceremony presided over by Valley great Billy Evans, a large contingent of "Niles' fans" who had traveled to the game gave a "rousing ovation as Mayor Crowe and Burns adjoined to home plate where the genial smile of the Niles mayor and the cheerful grin of the 'hero'"…was recorded for posterity by the Pathe Newsreel Motion Picture cameras. The date was October 12, 1920. The day before, Burns had made his boss look good by driving him across home plate in the sixth frame of Game Six of the World Series for the only score in a 1–0 Cleveland win against the National League champion Brooklyn Dodgers. In the aftermath of Hall of Fame player-manager Tris Speaker crossing home plate on Burns's lusty two-baser, the Indians basked in a four-games-to-two edge in the best-of-nine World

Series that year against opposing manager Wilbert Robinson's Dodgers. In that seventh game, Tribe rookie southpaw pitcher Walter "Duster" Mails, who hailed from San Quentin, California, took the win after completely shutting down Brooklyn's fabled Hall of Fame outfielder Zach Wheat and the rest of the Brooklyn hitters, pitching a five-hit complete game. For the crucial and potentially final Game Seven against Brooklyn's ace spitballer Burleigh Grimes, Speaker's pitching selection was clear and immediate, his own ace right-handed spitballer and future Hall of Famer Stan Coveleski, who had already scored victories for the Tribe in the series opener against fellow Hall of Famer Rube Marquard with a five-hit, 3–1 triumph and again in Game Four rematch against Marquard with another five-hit win, 5–1. Though he did not play in Game Seven, George Burns was likely the real hero of this contest. The first baseman, with his astute detective work from the bench, discovered how the Dodgers "telegraphed" their ace spitballer's throwing of his "wet pitch," giving his on-field teammates a distinct advantage in this crucial game.

And in Game Seven, before a sellout crowd of fifteen thousand fans at Cleveland's Dunn Field, Coveleski justified Speaker's faith by scattering yet another five hits in a 3–0 shutout against fellow Hall of Fame spitballer Grimes. Coveleski became just the seventh pitcher to reach the lofty circle

A team photo of the 1920 world champion Cleveland Indians. Players with ties to the Valley include pitcher George Uhle (*seated, first row, far left*), Stan Coveleski (*seated, first row, third from right*), Niles native George Burns (*second row, fourth from left*). The black armbands were worn in memory of slain shortstop Ray Chapman. *Cleveland Press Collection.*

The Cleveland Indians heroes of the 1920 World Series: George Henry Burns (*far right*) and Walter "Duster" Mails (*far left*). *Cleveland Press Collection.*

of winning three games in a single World Series, as the Cleveland Indians became the world champions with their fifth World Series win. Cleveland Indians owner "Sunny" Jim Dunn gushed, "I am the happiest man in the world today." In his front-page reporting, *Plain Dealer* sports editor Henry Edwards gave this very "un-woke-like" assessment: "On October 12, 1492, Christopher Columbus discovered America. On October 12, 1920, the Cleveland Indians—won the world's baseball championship." Edwards continued, "It was a long time to wait….For 42 years or more Cleveland has been striving to win a major league pennant. Year after year it was doomed to disappointment. Yesterday, Columbus Day, its ambitions were realized."

THE ROAD TO THE championship had been particularly difficult for Cleveland, marked by two horrific team tragedies. In the third inning of an August 16, 1920 road game, longtime Tribe shortstop Ray Chapman was struck in the head by a pitch thrown by New York Yankees submarine pitcher Carl Mays. Chapman, critically injured, was removed from the field and died early the next day after an emergency operation proved unsuccessful. Chapman's death remains to date the only on-field fatality in MLB history. The popular ballplayer was just twenty-nine years old. Earlier that year, on May 28, Stan Coveleski's world came crashing down as his wife of seven years, Mary Stivetts, died unexpectedly. "The heart broken pitcher immediately returned to his home in Shamokin, Pennsylvania to grieve with his family before returning to the team in June." Tribe manager Tris Speaker, in his first full year, deserved kudos for keeping the team focused and on point during this inordinately difficult period.

Speaker initiated an extensive use of "platooning" his position players during the run for the pennant, utilizing completely different lineups against right-handed pitchers and southpaws. To that end, Speaker acquired Valley great George Burns to bat against left-handed hurlers. Burns responded brilliantly in that role during the 1920 World Series.

Speaker also deserved praise for his clever use of his best pitchers: Stan Coveleski, who began the season red hot with seven consecutive victories before his personal tragedy occurred; Jim Bagby, who would end the season with thirty-one victories and 341 innings pitched; rookie right-hander George Uhle, who had ties to the Valley via the deft machinations of Dr. Reese; and World Series game winner Duster Mails. Speaker even managed to rein in the hard-throwing and harder-drinking right-hander Ray Caldwell by inserting a clause in his 1920 contract to get drunk immediately after his pitching assignment and subsequently abstain from alcohol for three days so that he would be sobered up for his next start. Speaker's gambit worked, and Caldwell contributed eighteen much-needed victories as the Indians outlasted Babe Ruth's New York Yankees and the soon-to-be infamous Chicago "Black" Sox, starring "Shoeless" Joe Jackson, to win the pennant.

Hall of Famer Tris Speaker is still considered the best defensive center fielder in baseball history as well as one of the absolute best hitters. Blasting two-basers was his specialty. Speaker led the league that year in that category with fifty. He was also his own team's best hitter, batting .388, scoring 137 runs and recording 107 RBIs.

Besides Speaker, perhaps the two players most instrumental in the Tribe's stunning World Series success that year were Mahoning Valley–born infielder George Burns, who batted .300, scored the first run of the series on a daring run from first base to home in Game One and won the penultimate contest with his clutch hitting; and star pitcher Stan Coveleski, who also had distinct ties to the Valley. In twenty-seven innings, Coveleski surrendered just two runs against the likes of Brooklyn's left fielder Wheat, first baseman Ed Konetchy and hard-hitting catcher Bing Miller. Another player with ties to the Mahoning Valley, right-handed pitcher George Uhle saw limited action in the World Series in a relief role.

George Henry Burns was born in Niles, Ohio, on January 31, 1893. His family moved from the Valley shortly after. As a boy, Burns honed his athletic skills on the back-alley sandlots of the Tioga section of Philadelphia and became known in the process as George "Tioga" Burns to help distinguish him from his contemporary, outfielder George Joseph Burns of the New York Giants in the National League. George H. Burns reached the majors in 1914 with the Detroit Tigers and compiled an excellent rookie season, batting .286. He played three seasons with the Tigers before being traded to Connie Mack's Philadelphia Athletics. With the A's, Burns had a breakout year in the war-shortened season of 1918. That year, Burns led the AL in hits (178) and total bases (236). He batted .352, finishing second in that category to Ty Cobb's .382. Burns also finished third in home runs and slugging percentage and came in second with seventy RBIs. By this time, he had acquired a second nickname, "General George," for his odd batting stance: standing straight at the plate with bat held high. Due to his stance and an inordinate willingness to visit the Mayo ward, Burns soon established yet another way to get to first: being hit by pitch. He remains among the all-time leaders in this category. Due to the aftereffects of a near-fatal bout with the Spanish flu, Burns had a disappointing season in 1919, which led to his trade to the Indians in their championship season of 1920.

Stan Coveleski had two separate but distinct ties to the Mahoning Valley. The spitballer was one of the scores of athletes who had his career extended by Youngstown's resident "miracle worker," Dr. John Reese. More important, Coveleski's eye-popping Hall of Fame pitching talent was discovered by none other than the legendary former Youngstown Ohio Works skipper Marty Hogan. Hogan, who always had a sharp eye for new talent, was managing

Overflow 1920 World Series crowd outside Cleveland's League Park. *Cleveland Press Collection.*

the 1909 Lancaster, Pennsylvania Red Roses club in the Tri-State League when he heard fantastic tales of a local Polish miner who could thread the eye of a needle with his fastball. In early spring, on one of the rare recreational off days on the "topside" of the mine, Stan Coveleski was watching a motion picture with his older brother John when a theater attendant walked to the front of the screen and loudly announced: "If Mr. Coveleski is in the house, he is wanted at the box office." Since neither brother knew who was being summoned, both left their seats and made their way to the box office, where Hogan was waiting. It was the younger Stan who was the target of the Lancaster manager. And despite Hogan's generous offer of $250 per month, far exceeding Coveleski's $9 per week salary at the mine, the unworldly and socially backward Stan would not sign until Hogan had also inked the elder John. It was Coveleski's first professional baseball contract. It would not be his last. With Coveleski as his ace, Marty Hogan led the Lancaster

Left: Stan Coveleski is pictured in 1925 after Cleveland's trade with the Washington Senators. Teaming with fellow Hall of Fame denizen Walter Johnson, both pitchers won twenty games to lead the D.C. ballclub to a repeat postseason appearance against the Pittsburgh Pirates. Pittsburgh won the 1925 championship in seven games. Coveleski suffered two losses. *Cleveland Public Library*.

Below: Dapper Mahoning Valley native George H. Burns (1893–1978). Burns is considered by many pundits to be the fourth-best first baseman in Cleveland Indians/Guardians history. *Author's collection*.

Red Roses to its first league pennant with a sparkling record of 75-39. Coveleski pitched 272 innings and led the league with twenty-three wins. Over time, Coveleski's four elder brothers pitched professionally, including Harry "The Giant Killer" Coveleski, who also reached the majors. Coveleski played again for Hogan in 1910 and compiled more dazzling statistics as the Red Roses had another truly excellent season but fell to second place in the league standings.

Born Stanislaus Kowalewski on July 13, 1889, in the coal-mining village of Shamokin, Pennsylvania, Stanley Anthony Coveleski honed his legendary pitching control as a boy, aiming rocks toward tin cans at a distance of sixty feet. His best pitch was his spitball. Although the pitch was outlawed in 1920, Coveleski was one of seventeen hurlers who were allowed to legally continue to throw the "wet one," as the rule was "grandfathered" in to allow this lucky group to finish their MLB careers. Coveleski's two seasons with Lancaster proved to be an advanced course for the quantum mechanics of applied baseball physics for the ex-miner, taught by genius professor Marty Hogan. Coveleski reached the majors with Connie Mack's Athletics in 1912, in just his second year after "graduation." Although the raw Coveleski pitched fairly well for the A's, Mack felt that the rookie needed more seasoning in the minors, which led to the Cleveland Indians' acquisition of Coveleski from Portland in 1916. During his second foray in the minors, Coveleski fine-tuned his soon-to-be-legendary spitball. With Cleveland, he began a string of eleven consecutive seasons of double-digit victories, including wins of 20 or more five times, 4 with the Indians and 1 with the Washington Senators in their pennant-winning season of 1925. In all, Coveleski pitched 38 career shutouts and finished with a career ERA of 2.89. On September 19, 1917, he pitched a one-hitter for the Tribe against the New York Yankees. Fritz Peterson ruined his bid for a no-hitter with a single in the seventh frame. Among the all-time Indians career leaders, Coveleski still ranks high in eight categories: 172 wins, 31 shutouts, a 2.80 ERA and a .583-win percentage. He pitched in 360 games, 2,503.3 innings, recorded 856 strikeouts and suffered 123 losses.

The discovery of the fabled Coveleski brothers was not Marty Hogan's only achievement in baseball. During his own short-lived MLB career, he set an all-time speed record to circle the bases. Born on October 25, 1869, in Wednesbury, England, the Olympic-caliber speedster made his MLB debut in 1894 with the Cincinnati Reds after batting .438 for the Akron Summits. Hogan was summarily traded to the St. Louis Browns late that same year after posting an abysmal .167 OPS in his first six games with the Reds. Hogan

The 1909 edition of the Lancaster Red Roses baseball team, featuring Marty Hogan (*standing, rear, fifth from left, with dark sweater*) and three of the five Coveleski brothers who played professional baseball: Stan (*fourth from left*), John (*third from left*) and Harry (*far left, with sweater*). *Mahoning Valley Historical Society.*

immediately became the Browns' primary outfielder to close out the season. In 1895, he was the Opening Day starter for the Browns but was again "farmed to Indianapolis in the Western League after collecting just three hits in five games." With the Hoosiers, Hogan became a huge gate attraction, sometimes racing a horse around the bases. In a pregame event on July 15, 1895, Hogan "beat Henry Buschman, the college sprint champion, in a 100-yard match race in which he was credited with tying the then official world record of 9.8 seconds. Later that summer, [Hogan] tied the record again in a match race at the Milwaukee ballpark and also set a new record of 13.2 seconds for circling the bases." Near the end of August, Hogan refused the Browns' offer to return to the parent club and, later, essentially "paid for his own release" from the Browns prior to the start of the 1896 season in order to return to the Hoosiers. A severe back injury soon after ended his MLB playing days prematurely after just forty career games. Hogan's injury proved to be severe, and the extensive convalescence took a toll on his health. For the better part of four years, the ballplayer was huddled near death with consumption and other maladies. In 1900, Hogan underwent

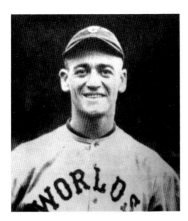

In the aftermath of his stellar 1926 MVP season, Burns was honored on May 2, 1927, at Cleveland's League Park (then known as Dunn Field). He received a silver bat stuffed with $1,150 and a motor car. *Author's collection.*

a successful operation to remove part of a rib. Over time, this seemed to restore his health enough to facilitate his return to baseball as a manager. Hogan became the skipper for the deep-pocketed Youngstown Ohio Works club in 1903. He remained at the helm until 1909, when he was hired to replace Pop Foster of the Lancaster, Pennsylvania franchise.

Another of Hogan's "finds" was "Sad" Sam Jones, who was pitching for Cleveland when he was traded on April 8, 1916, for Boston Red Sox centerfielder Tris Speaker. The trade included third baseman Fred Thomas and $55,000 to Boston. In 1913, Jones had played for Hogan with the Zanesville Flood Sufferers in the Interstate League. Like Stan Coveleski, Hogan inked Jones to his first professional baseball contract. Jones was a durable journeyman and pitched for two decades in the MLB with seven different teams, compiling a career record of 225-208.

Hogan remained a highly sought-after manager in low minor franchises. His teams were always competitive, and he was able to maximize talent on a shoestring budget. His managerial career was cut short. He died on August 15, 1923, in the aftermath of a horrific automobile accident. He was fifty-three years old.

It was perhaps "Sad" Sam Jones's greatest achievement in baseball, to be a part of the acquisition of Tris Speaker, which proved to be the single best trade in Cleveland history. Speaker performed brilliantly for the Tribe for eleven seasons, both offensively and defensively. He was also one of the franchise's most successful managers, serving from 1919 to 1926, during which his teams won 616 games while losing 520 for a .542 percentage. Speaker nearly brought home another pennant in 1926, his final season as Tribe manager, when the Valley's George Burns and pitcher George Uhle both had career years to bring Cleveland within three games of the best team in baseball history, the "Murderers' Row" lineup of the New York Yankees, with Babe Ruth, Lou Gehrig, Tony Lazzeri and pitcher Waite Hoyt. In 1926, Burns set a then-MLB record for doubles with sixty-four (since topped), batted .358, led the league in hits (216) and handily won the

The 1926 edition of the Cleveland Indians, surprise contenders for the American League flag. The team was led by three players with ties to the Valley, first baseman George Burns (*top row, second from left*), Benny Karr (*third row, far right, with sweater*) and George Uhle (*bottom row, far left*). *Cleveland Press Collection.*

The 1965 Cleveland Indians pitching staff, featuring the arms of, from left: Luis Tiant, Ralph Terry, Jack Kralick and "Sudden" Sam McDowell. Southpaw Mahoning Valley native Jack Kralick (1935–2012) led the Tribe with double-digit wins in 1964. *Cleveland Public Library.*

American League MVP award over Babe Ruth and Lou Gehrig. Uhle was almost as good, leading the league in wins (twenty-seven), complete games (twenty-three), innings pitched (318.1) and walks (118). Speaker resigned as manager at the end of the season.*

---

* In November 1927, Cleveland Indians owner Alva Bradley offered the New York Yankees first sacker George Burns plus $175,000 in a trade for an up-and-coming first baseman, Lou Gehrig. Yankees owner Ed Barrow summarily rejected Bradley's offer. The Tribe owner then increased the dollar amount to $250,000. The rest is history. Gehrig played his entire Hall of Fame career with the Yankees. Meanwhile, George Burns, age thirty-six, played part-time his final two years before retiring prior to the 1930 MLB season.

MAHONING VALLEY NEGRO LEAGUE STARS AND MODERN-DAY HEROES

Claude "Hooks" Johnson

Born: January 4, 1882, in Youngstown, Ohio
Died: January 5, 1961, in Youngstown, Ohio

Claude "Hooks" Johnson was a three-letter athlete in baseball, football and basketball in high school. He was the only man to captain Rayen and South baseball teams. After graduation, he played with local sandlot baseball teams. The second baseman extraordinaire was discovered by the genius Negro League player-manager "Candy" Jim Taylor. The 1920s Tate Stars were loaded with talent, including Fred Boyd, George Brown and Walter Cannady in the outfield; Don Hammond at third base; Willie Gray at first base; Pete Cordova at short; and pitchers Bob McClure, Slim Barnham Bill McCall and Square Moore. Moore played in Cleveland for six seasons, three with the Tate Stars; in 1926 with the Cleveland Elites; in 1927 with the Hornets; and in 1928 with the Tigers.

Hooks Johnson played with the Cleveland Tate Stars in 1921 and 1922 and was elevated to player-manager in 1923.

DIZZY DISMUKES

Born: March 15, 1890, in Birmingham, Alabama
Died: June 30, 1961, in Campbell, Ohio

This right-handed African American underhand submarine pitcher was considered a "trickster," due to the movement of his breaking balls. He is credited with a minimum 196 lifetime wins in the Negro Leagues. In 1911, Dismukes defeated the MLB Pittsburgh Pirates in an exhibition contest. In 1915, he hurled a no-hitter for the Indianapolis ABCs against the Chicago Giants at Northwestern Field. Reportedly, Dismukes taught the tricks of successful underhand pitching to fellow Negro Leaguer Webster McDonald and Carl Mays, whose errant fastball killed Indians shortstop Ray Chapman in 1920. Dismukes served with distinction in the 803rd Pioneer Infantry during World War I. His baseball career as player, manager, administrator and reporter spanned five decades (1910–51). In his later years, he was traveling secretary and, later, personnel director for the Kansas City Monarchs while moonlighting as the resident baseball columnist for the *Pittsburgh Courier*.

JOHN ALBERT KUCAB

Born: December 17, 1919, in Olyphant, Pennsylvania
Died: May 26, 1977, in Youngstown, Ohio

Kucab played three years in the majors after a long apprenticeship in the minors. He was a seldom-used right-handed relief power pitcher for the 1950 pennant-winning Philadelphia Phillies. The Phillies won ninety-one games to capture the National League flag that year, led by ace Hall of Famer Robin Roberts and fellow Cooperstown great, outfielder Richie Ashburn. Philadelphia was swept in the World Series by the New York Yankees. Kucab did not pitch in the Fall Classic that year. He continued his work with the Phillies through the 1951 and 1952 seasons. His best year was in 1951, when he recorded four relief wins and four saves.

Kucab was a combat veteran of World War II, serving in both the European and East Asian theaters. At the conclusion of his playing career, Kucab was employed by the Havanec Distribution Company in Youngstown.

GEORGE THOMAS "SHOTGUN" SHUBA

Born: December 13, 1924, in Youngstown, Ohio
Died: September 29, 2014, in Youngstown, Ohio

It was a golden, iconic, once-in-a-lifetime moment in baseball, a celebratory, spontaneous gesture between two teammates as one crossed the plate after a home run and was congratulated with a handshake.

The date was April 18, 1946, Opening Day for the Montreal Royals, the AAA farm club of the Brooklyn Dodgers. The game was a sellout, due to the presence of Jackie Robinson in the starting lineup, the first African American with the chance to play MLB baseball in the twentieth century. On October 23, 1945, Dodgers general manager Branch Rickey signed Robinson and designated the young speedster for a year of seasoning with the Royals the season following.

In his first at bat, Robinson grounded out, to cascading cheers and jeers. In the third, with two aboard, Robinson struck a titanic home run. Baseball etiquette requires the home-run hitter to be congratulated by the base runners as he touches home plate. In this case, both teammates snubbed Robinson and retreated to the safety of the dugout. Youngstown native George Shuba shattered baseball protocol, advancing from the on-deck circle to shake Robinson's hand as the African American crossed home plate. Both players smiled broadly in the heat of the moment, captured in a now-iconic photograph. The gesture was later deemed the "Handshake for the Century."

> *It was only a handshake,*
> *A bond between men.*
> *Teammate to teammate,*
> *That's all it was then.*
> *He stood there to greet him,*
> *Could've waited on deck.*
> *It was only a handshake,*
> *But it showed him respect.*
> *"The Handshake," song and lyrics by Chuck Brodsky, Asheville,*
> *North Carolina*

The careers of both men took wildly divergent paths after their moment of camaraderie. Robinson joined the Brooklyn Dodgers in 1947 and instantly became a star, his supreme talent forging a path to a first-ballot

1962 induction into baseball's Hall of Fame. Shuba was called up in 1948 as pinch-hitter and backup outfielder. Shuba remained in that role throughout his entire seven-year career. The Youngstowner was serious about his hitting, setting up a training area in his garage to practice his swings during the long winter off-season. The extra work paid off. Shuba became the first National Leaguer to pinch-hit a home run in a World Series.

In his lifetime, George Shuba was immortalized in Roger Kahn's paean to boyhood, *The Boys of Summer*, and is frequently reprinted. Seventy-five years after the fact, in 2021, *The Handshake for the Century* statue was unveiled at Wean Park near the Covelli Center, sculpted by the famed Marc Mellon.

The following updated essay first appeared in the *Review Newspapers* in 2007, shortly after the appearance of an Allen Ginter Topps baseball card (number 327), celebrating heretofore unknown stars of the Negro Leagues.

Ted Toles Jr.

Born: December 4, 1925, in Braceville, Ohio
Died: April 4, 2016, in Warren, Ohio

His hands are gnarled from a lifetime of hard work, but his voice and his words are still vigorous and strong, much like that day sixty-one years ago when he stared down one of the greatest teams in history, Black baseball's Pittsburgh Crawfords, and pitched a shutout for several innings. His name is Ted Toles, and he is a living monument to the greatness of the "blood and thunder era" that was once the Negro Leagues.

The Crawfords had a proud tradition in 1946 and were barnstorming across Ohio when they stopped in the Mahoning Valley for an exhibition contest against the lightly regarded local baseball stars. The game was set up by Charlie Caffie, a sports legend in his own right who had an ace up his sleeve: young pitching phenom Ted Toles of Braceville. Before the game, Caffie counseled Toles, telling him that if he pitched well that afternoon there would be a reward, but he gave no particulars. Toles then hurled shutout baseball. Inning after inning, his curveball nibbled at the corners of the strike zone. Effervescently calm despite the increasing crescendo of taunts from the visitors' bench, Toles pitched an expert game that day and was in command until the final out. After the contest, Caffie informed Toles that his performance had earned him a tryout with the Crawfords. The rest is history.

Toles was a true journeyman. From 1946 through 1950, he had stints with the Crawfords, the barnstorming Robinson All-Stars, the Cleveland Buckeyes and the Newark Eagles. From 1951 to 1953, Toles toiled for Saskatchewan, Canada; the New Castle Indians of Idaho; and affiliates of the New York Yankees and Philadelphia Athletics. One of his best days in baseball was on "Ted Toles Night," hosted by New Castle on July 21, 1951. "All my friends and family came over," Toles remembered. "It was a doubleheader, and we felt so confident, and the crowd was cheering….I had a home run and six hits in nine trips to the plate. That wasn't a bad day. That was one of the better days."

Toles was honored at several events during the 2006 All-Star Game ceremonies at the Highmark Legacy Square project inside the left-field entrance at PNC Park in Pittsburgh. Life-size bronze statues and interactive displays commemorating seven Negro League players from Pittsburgh were officially unveiled: Buck Leonard and Smokey Joe Williams of the Homestead Grays and Josh Gibson, "Cool Papa" Bell, Oscar Charleston and Satchel Paige of the Crawfords. Toles remains the last living ballplayer from this organization, his presence at the ceremony forming a link between past and present.

The Crawfords were founded in 1932 by Gus Greenlee, a numbers runner who named the team after his nightclub, the Crawford Grill Tavern in Pittsburgh. Greenlee successfully raided other Negro League teams, most notably the nearby Homestead Grays, and assembled an aggregate that many historians consider to be the greatest in baseball history. The team was built around powerhouse catcher Josh Gibson and, on the mound, Satchel Paige, whose array of breaking pitches coupled with a nasty curve and a legendary fastball made him the greatest drawing card in African American history. Gibson is believed to be the only ballplayer to hit a fair ball out of Yankee Stadium. Other players on the Crawfords included Hall of Famers third baseman Judy Johnson, Oscar Charleston, the fleet-footed "Cool Papa" Bell and Jimmy Crutchfield. The Crawfords won the Negro National League championship in 1935 and again in 1936. Greenlee later sold the team to Toledo. In 1945, the Crawfords were resurrected in the United States League, winning the title the following year. Most of the old-time Crawfords ended back with the crosstown Homestead Grays, forming a dynasty unparalleled in baseball. Many contemporary pundits felt it should have been Gibson and not Jackie Robinson to break baseball's color barrier. A Pennsylvania historical marker was presented in 1996 to pay tribute to Gibson at the site of the former Ammons Field and Hill District, where the Hall of Fame catcher played during his heyday.

JOSEPH CLIFFORD CAFFIE

Born: February 14, 1931, in Ramer, Alabama
Died: August 1, 2012, in Warren, Ohio

A somewhat quixotic model of consistency, the free-swinging outfielder batted left and threw right and maintained an excellent lifetime batting average of .291 in both the major and minor leagues. Caffie's eleven-year baseball career began in 1950 at the age of nineteen for the Cleveland Buckeyes in the Negro Leagues. He was one of only two ballplayers (with Quincy Trouppe) to play for both the Buckeyes and the Cleveland Indians. The Tribe signed the promising outfielder in 1951. Playing with Duluth in 1952, Caffie led the league in five categories: at bats, hits, triples, total bases and batting average. Caffie advanced to Indianapolis in the American Association and again led the league in several categories. During his peak years (1956–58), Caffie split time between Buffalo in the International League and the Cleveland Indians. With the Tribe in 1957, Caffie batted .270 and had three home runs in 890 at bats. Despite the stellar numbers, Caffie returned to Buffalo for the 1958 season. Playing three more years in the minors, Caffie never received another call-up to the parent club. At the conclusion of his playing days, he worked thirty-seven years at the Thomas Mill in Warren, Ohio.

WILLIAM DE KOVA WHITE

Born: January 28, 1934, in Lakewood, Florida

Born in Lakewood, Florida, White grew up in Warren, Ohio, and graduated from Warren G. Harding High School in 1958. He played MLB ball for the New York/San Francisco Giants, St. Louis Cardinals and Philadelphia Phillies. At Busch Stadium on May 7, 1956, White became one of the select few to hit a home run in his first MLB at bat. He was traded from San Francisco to St. Louis in March 1959. During his first season with St. Louis, White hit .302 and batted in seventy-two runs.

In 1960, White led the National League in double plays en route to winning his first Gold Glove Award. The year following, White tied the all-time mark for the most hits (fourteen) in consecutive doubleheaders, on July 17–18.

White played a total of thirteen years in the majors, with a lifetime batting average of .286, 870 RBIs, with 843 runs scored and 202 home runs. He became the president of the National League after his playing days ended.

W. James Cobbin

Born: December 27, 1934, in Montgomery, Alabama

Cobbin was a rangy outfielder who played exclusively in the Negro Leagues with the New York Black Yankees and the Indianapolis Clowns in 1956–57, the two premier African American teams of the era. The Clowns were especially selective in assembling its roster, a tribute to Cobbin's talent and versatility. In 1952, the Clowns signed seventeen-year-old future Hall of Famer Hank Aaron. The Clowns also signed the first professional female ballplayer, Toni Stone, in 1951. Her success led to two additional signings in 1954, Connie Morgan and Mamie "Peanuts" Johnson.

Cobbin currently lives in Youngstown, Ohio, and remains one of a select few Negro League stars still living.

John Francis Kralick

Born: June 1, 1935, in Youngstown, Ohio
Died: September 18, 2012, in San Blas, Nayarit, Mexico

Southpaw Jack Kralick pitched nine seasons in the major leagues for the Minnesota Twins, Washington Senators and Cleveland Indians. He compiled a 67-65 career record and was selected to the All-Star Game in 1964.

He was known for pitching no-hitters. On August 26, 1962, Kralick, pitching for the Minnesota Twins, threw a tough 1–0 no-hitter against the Kansas City Athletics.

On July 17, 1955, he threw his first no-hitter as a professional in the Kitty League for the Madison (Kentucky) Miners over the Union City Dodgers. The game was halted in the seventh inning.

On August 8, 1956, Kralick followed up a year later, pitching a no-no for the Duluth Superior White Sox against Fargo Moorhead in the Northern League. This game was also halted after the conclusion of the seventh frame.

The 1999 edition of the Mahoning Valley Scrappers take the field. The last minor-league team prior to the Scrappers was the Youngstown Athletics, playing at Idora Park. Baseball at the Y'town amusement park dated from the 1930s, with infielder Floyd Baker (1916–2004) as the most illustrious alumni. *Mahoning Valley Scrappers.*

On May 26, 1958, at the National Semi Pro Tournament in Wichita, the left-hander added another no-hitter pitching for Grand Rapids, Michigan, against Slagboom Construction.

When his playing career ended, Kralick became a sport angler in the coastal town of San Blas in Mexico until his death in 2012.

HAROLD EUGENE RENIFF

Born: July 2, 1938, in Warren, Ohio
Died: September 4, 2004, in Ontario, Canada

Though born in Warren, the Reniff family moved to Ontario in 1948. Reniff played his entire MLB career with New York City teams, primarily the Yankees (1961–67). In 1967, he closed out his career with a twenty-nine-game stint with the New York Mets. Reniff's debut season was memorable to the extreme, giving the Warren native a front-row seat to the fabled rise of the "M&M" boys, when Hall of Fame outfielder Mickey Mantle and former Tribesman Roger Maris battled to beat Babe Ruth's single-season home run record, with Maris blasting sixty-one in 1961 on the final day.

The right-handed middle reliever also played in two World Series, 1963 and 1964. In all, Reniff had forty-five career saves and posted a very respectable 3.27 lifetime ERA.

EDWIN MARVIN STROUD

Born: October 31, 1939, in Lapine, Alabama
Died: July 2, 2012, in Cleveland, Ohio

He was called the "Ghost" for his base-stealing prowess—the streak of the base paths. He also acquired the nom de guerre the "Creeper" for his most unusual walk. His name was Ed Stroud. Stroud's speed in the outfield and his skill and savvy for extending singles into doubles and triples translated into a seven-year major league career. He was born in Lapine, Alabama, and Stroud's family moved to Warren, Ohio, when he was still a toddler. Stroud loved the area and lived in the Mahoning Valley for about seventy years. He graduated from Warren G. Harding High School in 1958 and then served in the U.S. Army for two years.

Signed by the Chicago White Sox in 1963, Stroud ran amok in his professional debut with Clinton that year, stealing seventy-four bases to lead the Midwestern League and tallied 119 runs in 124 games. The following season with the Portsmouth Tidewater Tides, the speedster batted .323, swiped seventy-two bags and was named the Carolina League MVP. Stroud continued to burn up the minor leagues, culminating with fifty-seven purloined bases for the Triple A Indianapolis Indians in the Pacific Coast League and leading to a late-season debut with the Chicago White Sox on September 11, 1966. The following year, Stroud was batting .309 when he was traded to the lowly Washington Senators on June 15, 1967. Stroud instantly became a regular in the Senators outfield for the next several seasons (1967–70). The left-handed batter enjoyed perhaps his finest day at the plate on July 4, 1968, when he struck a pair of doubles and two triples, leading his team to a 4–2 victory over the much-hated New York Yankees. That year, Stroud and teammate Frank Howard supplied most of the offensive fireworks for the Senators. Howard led the American League in home runs, blasting forty-four, while Stroud reached double digits with ten triples, finishing third in that category. Despite their personal heroics, the D.C. club finished in the cellar, even below the fledgling Minnesota Twins and California Angels.

Baseball was a-changing in 1969 with the institution of a lower pitching mound, reduced to ten inches; a shrunken strike zone; and the expansion Seattle Pilots and Kansas City Royals in the American League and the San Diego Padres and the Montreal Expos in the National League. The Senators unveiled changes of their own, with a new owner, Bob Short, and a new manager, first-ballot Hall of Fame inductee Ted Williams, as well as newly styled uniforms. Lumped into the AL Eastern Division, the Nats were scheduled to play ninety games against the five best teams in the league: the Yankees, Red Sox, Tigers, Orioles and Indians. Pundits widely predicted that the temperamental Williams would not last the season and that the awful Washington club would sport the worst record in baseball. Instead, after a rocky start, the Senators blossomed to win eighty-six games, one of the finest seasons in their long history. Ted Williams was named Manager of the Year. Stroud was an integral part of that "Cinderella" season of 1969. The following year, the "Creeper" put together perhaps his best MLB season, with twenty-nine steals and a batting average of .266.

Ed Stroud was traded back to the Chicago White Sox prior to the start of the 1971 season. He played his final MLB game on June 29, 1971. Stroud remained in the Mahoning Valley at the conclusion of his playing career. He became the Equal Opportunity Coordinator for the city of Warren until his 1998 retirement. Baseball remained in his blood, thought, and Stroud became a fixture on the area softball circuit, playing with fellow ex-major-leaguer Darrin Chapin and with Rob Dipofi, pitching extraordinaire Joe Lamanna, Dennis Havalcheck, Mark Morgan and Donnie Kirkwood.

DAVID CHRISTOPHER RAJSICH

Born: September 28, 1951, in Youngstown, Ohio

The bespectacled, mustachioed, southpaw pitcher was the older brother of Gary Rajsich. He played for the New York Yankees and the Texas Rangers from 1978 through 1980. He also played one year (1984) in the Japanese League with the Hiroshima Toyo Carp. He was known as the "Blade" because of the differential of his height (six foot, five inches) to his weight (175 pounds).

Although both brothers played for the Yankees, they were not teammates. Dave played in Gotham in 1978, while Gary wore the pinstripes in 1982–83.

JOHN ANDREW KUCEK

Born: June 8, 1953, in Newton Falls, Ohio

Right-handed legendary fastball pitcher Jack Kucek played for the Chicago White Sox, Philadelphia Phillies and Toronto Blue Jays. He was twice drafted by the White Sox and spent the majority of his career with that organization. Throughout his seven-year career, Kucek split time between the majors and the minors.

At the start of his MLB career, he was a starter but eventually was used primarily in relief roles. As a reliever, his lifetime record was 2-2 with two saves.

He played with Wilbur Wood, Steve Stone, Oscar Gamble, Lloyd Moseby, John Mayberry, Alfredo Griffin and Damasco Garcia.

GEORGE ANGELO CAPPUZZELLO

Born: January 15, 1954, in Youngstown, Ohio

Southpaw pitcher Cappuzzello played professional baseball for eleven seasons, including two full seasons in the majors with the Detroit Tigers and Houston Astros, averaging five strikeouts per game. Cappuzzello made his MLB debut on May 31, 1981. For the Tigers, he started three games, relieved fifteen and posted an excellent 3.48 ERA for the season. He was traded in the off-season to the Astros, who had one of the best pitching staffs of the era. Hall of Famers Nolan Ryan and Don Sutton were on the team, along with Joe Niekro. Though seldom used, Cappuzzello posted impressive numbers. In nineteen innings, he gave up just sixteen hits, struck out thirteen and posted a 2.79 ERA.

GARY LOUIS RAJSICH

Born: October 28, 1954, in Youngstown, Ohio

Left-handed batter and brother of Dave Rajsich, Gary played for the New York Yankees, St. Louis Cardinals and San Francisco Giants. Gary also played in the Japanese League with the Chunichi Dragons for three seasons (1985–88). In 1989, he played in the Senior Professional Baseball Association with the St. Petersburg Pelicans.

Although both brothers played for the Yankees, Gary and Dave were not teammates. Gary played for New York in 1982–83, and Dave played in 1978. Gary Rajsich became a bird dog of some renown when his playing career ended.

David Francis Dravecky

Born: February 14, 1956, in Youngstown, Ohio

Therefore, do not lose heart. Though outwardly we are wasting away,
inwardly we are being rewarded day by day. For our light and momentary
troubles are achieving for us an eternal glory that far outweighs them all.
—2 Corinthians 4:16–17

It was the "pitch heard 'round the world." On August 10, 1989, the San Francisco Giants were playing the Montreal Expos. Southpaw Giants hurler Dave Dravecky was back on the hill, the subject of worldwide attention. Less than one year after cancer surgery on his pitching arm, Dravecky was beating the odds and the removal of much of his deltoid muscle, pitching like he had never been away. A deeply religious man who lived out his faith in God, Dravecky seemed at peace with the vagaries of his affliction and had bravely soldiered on after surgery, winning his first start five days earlier. At Expos/Olympic Stadium facing opposing batter Tim Raines, Dravecky felt his arm snap, his bone broken. He fell to the ground in pain, his MLB baseball career at an end. Yet almost immediately, Dravecky realized that his baseball career had been a mere "stepping stone to something greater." Within a year, doctors had removed his left arm and shoulder, providing the fodder for his first two best-selling inspirational books, *Comeback* and *When You Can't Come Back*. "Baseball is actually a tool to remind me of the faithfulness of God," Dravecky said. Dravecky finished his eight-year MLB career with a lifetime 64-57 record and an excellent 3.13 ERA.

The San Francisco Giants reached the World Series in 1989 but were swept in four games by the Oakland Athletics. The World Series was notable for the interruption by an earthquake that delayed the finale until October 28, at that point the latest finish in MLB history.

Darrin Chapin

Born: February 1, 1966, in Warren, Ohio

Chapin, a right-handed knuckleballer, played for the New York Yankees and Philadelphia Phillies. The Warrenite played with some of the greatest players of the era, including Don Mattingly, Steve Sax, Jesse Barfield,

Longtime Scrappers manager Travis Fryman, a former Cleveland Indians great. *Mahoning Valley Scrappers*.

Scrappy with friends. Over time, Scrappy has been the most prolific autograph hound—er, bulldog—in Mahoning Valley Scrappers history, putting his paw print on thousands of baseball cards and various other forms of Scrappers memorabilia. *Mahoning Valley Scrappers*.

Above: Scrappers fireball pitcher Carston Charles "C.C." Sabathia has an excellent chance at induction into the Cooperstown baseball Hall of Fame. A six-time All-Star with 256 career wins, the southpaw is one of only eleven hurlers to surpass 3,000 strikeouts, reaching 3,104 in a career that spanned sixteen years. *Mahoning Valley Scrappers*.

Left: The 2010 Scrappers great Gio Urshela. The six-foot right-handed third baseman from Cartagena, Colombia, first reached the majors in 2015. The well-traveled infielder has also played for the Toronto Blue Jays, the New York Yankees and the Minnesota Twins. *Mahoning Valley Scrappers*.

Kevin Maas and pitchers Eric Plunk, Steve Howe and Pascual Perez of the Yankees. He also played with Dale Murphy, Wally Backman, Lenny Dykstra and pitchers Kurt Schilling, Mitch Williams and Terry Mulholland of the Phillies. In their only matchup, Chapin struck out Hall of Famer Tony Gwynn. Chapin was drafted by the Yankees in Round 6 out of Community College in Cuyahoga County.

At the conclusion of his baseball career, Chapin remained in the Valley and became a familiar sight on the Valley's softball fields, playing with fellow major-leaguer Ed Stroud.

16

"WE WANT BASEBALL! WE WANT BASEBALL!"

*But baseball has marked time with America....It continually reminds us
of what once was.*
—*W.P. Kinsella, Shoeless Joe*

This is a wonderful Park....It's a long time coming.
—*Michele Gulas*

As always, it was the naysayers who first ruled the microphone. In early 1998, Al Levine, the managing general partner of Palisades Baseball Ltd., first proposed relocating the Erie Seawolves franchise to the Mahoning Valley. If successful, it would mark the return of minor league baseball after a hiatus of four decades. To that end, the Cambridge Investment Group of Cleveland, headed by Sam and Greg Moffie, approached the Niles City Council with an eye-popping $4.5 million bid to utilize the fallow woodland acreage that abutted the city's Eastwood Mall complex for the construction of a state-of-the-art minor league baseball stadium. Their endeavor had the backing of U.S. representative James Traficant (D-Ohio).

Surprisingly to some, the Moffies' proposal was later rebuffed by the city, deemed too financially risky. Shortly after, the mall-building Cafaro Company, headquartered squarely within the Valley, offered a tantalizing counterproposal, Niles would be responsible for $1 million "in infrastructure, improvements, material, labor and the waiver of fees," while the Cafaro Company would be the sole private investor for the estimated $7.5 million stadium and would bear the responsibility for the day-to-day maintenance of the facility, with no subsequent liability to Niles.

In a March 12, 1998 Niles city newspaper op ed, the *Times* columnist Michelle Monteforte-Gray wrote the following in her *Shades of Gray* feature: "I don't blame City Council for refusing to…deal with the Moffie brothers.… In my mind, that deal held little risk for the Moffies but a great deal of risk for the city. I wouldn't have voted for it either.

"But this latest deal with the Cafaro Co. seems fair to all concerned."

Yet many in the area remained opposed to the project, and more than a few were vehemently against it. Their concerns focused primarily on the enormous cost. The naysayers soon flooded the radio waves and were prolific in a concerted letter-to-the-editor campaign directed at the local newspaper outlets. The money wasted on this ill-fated venture could be better spent elsewhere in the community and to greater effect.

The veritable tsunami of negative commentary did not go unnoticed to "Uberfans" John Brown of Warren, Ohio, his sons George and Johnnie and his father, John Sr., who witnessed with horror their wonderful "Field of Dreams" slipping away. In response, John Brown arranged a 6:00 p.m. rally on Friday, March 27, 1998, at the local BW3 restaurant to save the team, open to the Valley's legion of baseball fans. The event was heavily promoted in print and on the local airwaves, notably Sal Marino's *Yours in Sports* broadcast on the now-defunct 1570 radio station. Again, lending his considerable support was U.S. Representative James Traficant.

On the day of the event, John Brown remembered driving to the venue approximately forty-five minutes before the start. He was pleasantly surprised by the presence of satellite trucks in the parking lot for each of the three local television networks: WFMJ 21, WKBN 27 and WYTV 33. Scant minutes later, fans began arriving in droves, their cars forming an impromptu caravan. It soon became clear that the mass of humanity was too large for the venue. "It was chaos," he recalled.

As agreed, Representative Traficant arrived at 6:10 p.m. to say a few words in his inimitable style. As the congressperson started to speak, the crowd loudly chanted, "We want baseball! We want baseball!" The spontaneous outpouring of sentiment, carried live via satellite, was viewed in real time by William M. Cafaro, who had in the chamber of his executive office three televisions tuned to each of the news affiliates. The eighty-four-year-old patriarch of the family-owned Cafaro enterprise hurriedly phoned son Anthony, telling him to turn on his TV. "Which channel?" Anthony inquired. "All of them!"

The timing of the broadcast could not have been more fortuitous. Earlier that day, in the wake of such vociferous opposition, the Cafaro family had reluctantly decided to reverse course and abandon the stadium project. The announcement was scheduled to be formally drafted the week following. The naysayers had won. Brown's brilliantly staged ballyhoo had turned the trick, and the Cafaro family was again firmly on board. The rally had indeed succeeded in changing forever the course of history. And in short order, construction for the six-thousand-seat stadium began. Palisades Baseball Ltd. named Andy Milovich general manager, and on November 26, 1998, came the official announcement: the area team, named the Mahoning Valley Scrappers, would replace Watertown, New York as the Cleveland Indians' New York Penn League Class A short season affiliate. The official mascot was a comically fierce-looking bulldog in a hard hat named "Scrappy."

William M. Cafaro would not live to see his beloved stadium project to fruition. On April 22, 1998, the family patriarch died of heart failure at his office, a visionary workaholic to the end. At the time of his death, the elder leader of the Cafaro family was listed among the four hundred richest Americans by *Forbes* magazine, while the privately held Cafaro Company ranked in the top ten of commercial real estate developers in America. The final cost of the stadium was an estimated $8 million. And in tribute to his final project, the Mahoning Valley Scrappers would play at Cafaro Field.

On Friday, June 25, 1999, Cafaro Field opened to a sellout crowd of 6,718 fans. The Mahoning Valley Scrappers hosted the Auburn Doubledays. *Beacon Journal* staff writer David Lee Morgan Jr. characterized the proceedings as a "big league atmosphere in a minor league ballpark," complete with an impressive fireworks display after the game. With the Budweiser blimp flying overhead and ballpark concessionaires selling their fares dressed in construction gear garb, the mascot Scrappy entered the field in pregame style—a stretch limousine with a tune by rapper Snoop Dogg blaring over the loudspeaker system. Just prior to the first pitch, a crack team of military-style parachuters fell from the sky, landing near home plate. And without further ado, eighteen-year-old, six-foot, six-inch southpaw fireballer Carsten Charles "C.C." Sabathia took the hill for the Mahoning Valley Scrappers. Drafted right out of his Vallejo, California high school, Sabathia was the Cleveland Indians' first-round pick in the June 1998 draft. His presence on the team was ceremonial, and C.C. exited after three quick innings.

In every way, the home opener proved to be worthy of the Scrappers' name. Down by two runs in the bottom of the eighth inning with no outs, the Scrappers mounted an impressive come-from-behind victory when

Above: A familiar scene: a Scrappers sellout crowd at Eastwood Field in Niles, Ohio. *Mahoning Valley Scrappers*.

Left: The perennial fan favorite, All-Star 2011 Scrappers alumni Francisco Lindor, is in many ways the ultimate Believeland Indians star. On Opening Day 2021, Lindor became baseball's $341 million man, as the popular shortstop signed a ten-year contract with the New York Mets. *Mahoning Valley Scrappers*.

switch-hitting Venezuelan catcher Victor Martinez blasted a sharp daisy-cutter single to drive home one run. He later scored the go-ahead tally on teammate Curtis Gay's two-base "buttercup thumper." A bases-loaded walk scored another run, followed by a bases-loaded hit-by-pitch. The Scrappers won by a score of 8–5 for the first ever victory on their home turf. The impressive postgame fireworks display insured that the sellout crowd remained in their seats in celebration after the game.

John Brown and his family remained die hard Mahoning Valley Scrappers fans. Sons George and Johnnie later became bat boys while John himself for many years conceived and promoted a quasi "Foster Family Program" for the annual revolving door of Scrappers ballplayers, pairing them with selected Mahoning Valley families to provide food, lodging and transportation during off days and home games. Brown is currently an usher during Scrapper's home games.*

---

* The last minor-league team located in the Mahoning Valley prior to the Scrappers was the 1951 Youngstown Athletics, who played at Idora Park. Baseball at the amusement park dated from the 1930s, with infielder Floyd Baker as its most illustrious alumnus. Known as a light-hitting glove man, Baker played with the St. Louis Browns, Chicago White Sox, Washington Senators and Philadelphia Phillies. He played briefly in the 1944 World Series for the Browns when they squared off against the cross-town Cardinals. Born in the town of Luray, Virginia, Baker had a lifetime batting average of a mere .251; however, his defensive prowess, coupled with an uncanny ability to fatten his on-base percentage with his keen batting eye and ability to coax bases on balls, stretched an otherwise light-hitting talent into a sparkling thirteen-year career. After his retirement as a player following the 1955 season, Baker remained in the game as a scout for the Minnesota Twins until 1995. His most famous signings were Bernie Allen, Richie Rollins, Lamar "Jake" Jacobs, Joe Nossek and Garry Roggenburk. Born in 1916, Baker died in Youngstown on November 16, 2004.

17

THE SCRAPPERS' GREATEST YEAR

THE 2016 "BELIEVELAND" INDIANS

He's just a special kid.
—Cleveland Indians manager Terry Francona on Francisco Lindor,
to Tom Withers, Associated Press, October 25, 2016

A Wrigley home run. A World Series home run.
There's so many things you could check off.
—Chicago native Jason Kipnis to Marla Ridenour, Akron Beacon Journal,
October 31, 2016

I don't remember too much....I knew it was a home run,
so I slowed down pretty quickly.
—Lonnie Chisenhall to Marla Ridenour, Akron Beacon Journal,
October 8, 2016

*I*t was October 1, 2016, at Kauffman Stadium in Kansas City, Missouri. In the ninth inning of an otherwise meaningless game, the Cleveland Indians were leading the Kansas City Royals by score of 6–3 when Mahoning Valley Scrappers alumni Jesus Aguilar took the field, replacing Tribe first baseman Mike Napoli. The twenty-six-year-old Venezuelan joined former and future Scrappers infielders Francisco Lindor at shortstop, Jason Kipnis at second base, Jose Ramirez at third, Tyler Naquin in center field, Coco Crisp in left field and Lonnie Chisenhall in right. Onetime Mahoning Valley hurler Cody Allen took the hill and later recorded his thirty-first save. Allen's battery mate that inning was Yan Gomes, the only player on the field who had never played in the Mahoning Valley. Catcher Roberto Perez, a graduate of the Scrappers' class of 2009, had been replaced for a pinch-runner in the eighth inning. And for the first (and last) time in MLB history, Mahoning Valley Scrappers alumni had, at various points, taken the field for all nine positions in a single game. In all, twenty-one former Scrappers dotted the roster of the 2016 Cleveland Indians: pitchers Cody Allen (2011), Cody Anderson (2011), Sean Armstrong (2011), Joe Colon (2011), Kyle Crockett (2013), T.J. House (2014), Ryan Merritt (2014), Dan Otero (2019), Danny Salazar (2017) and Josh Tomlin (2006); catchers Roberto Perez (2009) and Chris Gimenez (2004); infielders Jesus Aguilar (2010), Eric Gonzalez (2012), Francisco Lindor (2011), Jason Kipnis (2009) and Jose Ramirez (2012); and outfielders Michael Brantley (2016) (on a rehab assignment in 2016), Lonnie Chisenhall (2008), Coco Crisp (2020) and Tyler Naquin (2012).

The 2016 American League pennant race had ended days before, with the unexpected ascendancy of the Tribe over the 2015 world champion Royals in the AL Central Division. The Royals were expected to "threepeat" as champions of their division under manager Ned Yost. Despite the loss of several free agents, the champions maintained a superior lineup, with Lorenzo Cain, Eric Hosmer, Kendrys Morales, Mike Moustakas and pitchers Wade Davis, Chris Young and Jason Vargas. But it was the Tribe that prevailed due to the Svengali workmanship of manager Terry Francona, who effectively utilized a revolving door of former Scrappers to win close games and take home the American League Central Division title. Non-Scrappers players included ace right-hander Cory Kluber and southpaw long reliever Andrew Miller, added in a midseason trade with the New York Yankees to the already "lights-out" relief corps led by closer and former Scrapper Cody Allen. These players helped vault the Indians to represent the Central Division against the Boston Red Sox in the first round of the American League Division Series (ALDS).

The heavily favored Red Sox were loaded with talent, starting with their forty-year-old powerful Goliath of a designated hitter, future Hall of Famer David Ortiz, and a roster of Mookie Betts, Justin Pedroia and Xander Bogaerts. Their starting pitching was also deep, with the newly acquired David Price, Clay Buchholz and Rick Porcello. The teams crossed bats at Progressive Field on October 6, 2016, for Game One of the ALDS. In the bottom of the third inning, with the Sox nursing a slim 2–1 lead, three former Scrappers launched solo home runs within the span of nine pitches to break the backs of the heavily favored Red Sox. On a three-and-two count, catcher Roberto Perez, who had batted a lowly .183 during the regular season, blasted a home run against Rick Porcello to tie the score. Five pitches later, with one down, Jason Kipnis parked a souvenir into the bleachers beyond the center-field First Energy sign. This was followed by rookie shortstop Francisco Lindor, who lined a shot over the wall on a 1-0 count to finish the barrage. Perez scored again in the fifth for the deciding run as the Tribe won the opener, 5–4. In Game Two, former Scrapper Lonnie Chisenhall hit a three-run homer in the second frame to give Cory Kluber all the firepower he needed in his 6–0 shutout win. And in the finale, Mahoning Valley great Coco Crisp homered in the winning run in a 4–3 victory for alumni Scrappers hurler Josh Tomlin. With their stunning David-over-Goliath victory, "Believeland" was born. It was a Cinderella season for the Tribe. All things wondrous were possible, even a trip to the World Series ball.

Believeland's pixie dust continued in the opener of the American League Championship Series (ALCS) against the Toronto Blue Jays, when Lindor cleared the bases with a two-run blast in the sixth frame, scoring fellow Scrappers alumni Jason Kipnis to provide all the scoring as Cory Kluber pitched a 2–0 shutout win. Former Scrappers star Cody Allen pitched a perfect ninth for the save.

Three former Scrappers combined their talents to score a Tribe victory in Game Two. Starter Josh Tomlin pitched six strong innings, Lindor had a game-winning single in the Tribe third and Cody Allen recorded his second consecutive save in a 2–1 Cleveland victory. Perhaps more than any other, the perpetually smiling Lindor had become a true believer, with "Believeland" boldly etched on his sneakers, framed with the Cleveland skyline in the backdrop. The Tribe won the ALCS four games to one, with Scrappers great Coco Crisp hitting a home run in the finale and Cody Allen getting his third save.

Believeland was in the World Series against the Chicago Cubs.

The 2016 World Series was a battle of the "Curses." Cleveland's "Colavito Curse" originated in 1960, when fan favorite Rocky Colavito was traded to the Detroit Tigers. The Chicago's "Billy Goat Curse" dated from the 1945 World Series, when Windy City tavern owner Billy Sianis and his pet goat Murphy were booted from Wrigley Field after causing a disturbance. Sianis angrily stood in the parking lot and proclaimed, "Them Cubs, they ain't gonna win no more." His prophecy had proven accurate. The last time the Cubs had won the World Series was 1908. Equally, the Colavito Curse hexed the Indians in their World Series losses of 1995 against the Atlanta Braves and again in 1997 versus the Miami Marlins, when the Tribe lost Game Seven in extra innings. The last time the Indians had won the World Series was 1948.

On October 25, the hometown Believeland Indians squared off against the Chicago Cubs in Game One of the 2016 World Series at Progressive Field as 38,091 fans watched. The pitchers were Cory Kluber for the Tribe and Jon Lester of the Cubs. In this game, former Scrappers star Roberto Perez became the first native-born Puerto Rican to hit two home runs in World Series history. Jose Ramirez notched an RBI single, and Cody Allen finished the game, a 6–0 Tribe win.

In Game Two at Progressive Field, the adage "Good pitching always beats good hitting" was illustrated by Cubs pitcher Jake Arrieta, as he completely cooled off the red-hot bats of the Indians by pitching a no-hitter for five innings (until Valley star Jason Kipnis doubled in the sixth and later scored the Tribe's only run). Believeland's magic was strangely absent in a 5–1 defeat, with Trevor Bauer taking the loss.

Game Three moved to Wrigley Field in Chicago on October 28. The starting pitchers were Scrappers favorite Josh Tomlin and Cubs right-hander Kyle Hendricks. The game proved to be a real pitchers' duel, as the game's only score was an RBI single off the bat of future Scrappers favorite Coco Crisp in the seventh. Cody Allen struck out Javier Baez with two aboard in the ninth to preserve a tight 1–0 Believeland win for Allen's sixth postseason save.

In Game Four at Wrigley Field, Chicago native Jason Kipnis hit a three-run homer in the seventh inning that finished the home team in a 7–2 bloodbath as Believeland's magic returned with a vengeance. Cory Kluber recorded his second World Series win. The Tribe was one win shy of victory with three games to play.

In the Game Five finale at Wrigley on October 30, Francisco Lindor singled home a run in the sixth frame to bring the Tribe within a run of tying the game, but the Cubs ultimately won, 3–2, as Cubs fireballer Aroldis Chapman shut out Believeland's bats for two and a half innings. Jon Lester got the win, and Trevor Bauer took the loss. Scrappers favorite Jose Ramirez blasted an Indians home run in the second inning.

Game Six, on November 1, moved back to Cleveland's Progressive Field before 38,116 fans. In this game, second baseman Jason Kipnis blasted his second World Series home run, and Roberto Perez had an RBI single. It was not enough. Former Scrappers starter Josh Tomlin gave up three quick runs in the first frame then loaded the bases in the third. Fellow Mahoning Valley alumni reliever Dan Otero then took the hill, facing Addison Russell. Russell promptly cleared the bases with a grand slam. Cubs pitcher Jake Arrieta recorded his second World Series victory, and Tomlin absorbed the 9–3 loss.

For both teams, it was do or die for the seventh game, and for one, an abominable curse would be forever lifted. The date was November 2, 2016. With 38,104 fans crammed into Progressive Field and thousands more outside the ballpark, the faithful watched with horror as batter Dexter Fowler homered for the Cubs in the first. Later, Javier Baez finished Tribe starter Cory Kluber with a home run in the fifth. The inning following, the Cubs' ancient mariner, catcher David Ross, parked a solo shot into deep center field as the Cubs built a 6–3 lead. Ross's blast atoned for his earlier blunder in the fifth that allowed Kipnis and Carlos Santana to score on a throwing error. Neither team scored in the seventh.

In the Tribe eighth, Cubs pitcher Jon Lester, used in a relief role in this game, dispatched Lindor and struck out Mike Napoli. Lester was removed for fireballer Aroldis Chapman after giving up a single to Jose Ramirez. It was here that the Tribe's Believeland pixie dust was delivered one last time from the inscrutable gods of baseball. Down by three runs with two outs, on a full count, Tribe batter Brandon Guyer doubled home Ramirez. The score was now Chicago 6, Cleveland 4. Next up was centerfielder Rajai Davis, who was hitless in this game and batting .132 during the postseason. Davis worked Chapman to a two-and-two count, then hit a home run that cleared (barely) the left-field wall to tie the game at six.

The Cubs put runners on base in the ninth with two outs, and Dexter Fowler hit a line drive that looked to be a game winner. But it was not to be. A spectacular catch by shortstop Francisco Lindor sent the contest into extra innings. Before the tenth inning could begin, the skies opened up and a hard rain forced a seventeen-minute delay, which pushed the finish into the following day.

The delay seemed to swing the momentum back to the Cubs. And indeed, in the top of the tenth, Cubs batter Kyle Schwarber led off with a single off reliever Bryan Shaw. Schwarber was immediately replaced for a pinch runner, Albert Almora. Almora tagged up on Kris Bryant's long fly out and advanced to second base. Shaw intentionally walked the next batter, Anthony Rizzo. Ben Zobrist followed with a clutch double that scored Almora. Shaw then issued another intentional walk to Addison Russel to get to the lightly regarded Miguel Montero. Unfortunately, Montero came through, singling

Above: Soon after his late-season arrival, the switch-hitting thirty-six-year-old 2020 Scrappers alumni Coco Crisp became a star for the 2016 edition of the Believeland Indians. The fifteen-year MLB veteran led the AL in batting with runners in scoring position that year with a .392 average. *Mahoning Valley Scrappers.*

Right: The 2012 Scrappers alumni Tyler Naquin played 116 games for the 2016 Believeland Indians, batting .296. The center fielder scored fifty-two runs that year with forty-three RBIs. *Mahoning Valley Scrappers.*

Top: The 2014 Scrappers alumni Greg Allen reached the majors with Cleveland in 2017. The six-foot switch-hitting outfielder has played on four teams: the New York Yankees, San Diego Padres and the Pittsburg Pirates in addition to the Tribe. *Mahoning Valley Scrappers*.

Bottom: Scrappers alumni Joey Wendle reached the majors in 2016 with the Oakland Athletics. The versatile infielder was born on April 26, 1990, in Wilmington, Delaware, the adopted hometown of another famed person named Joe: the forty-sixth president of the United States, Joe Biden. *Mahoning Valley Scrappers*.

Left: Scrappers alumni Bradley Zimmer was nicknamed "The Machine" by his teammates. Former Scrappers pitcher Josh Tomlin explained: "He's huge [six foot, five inches and 220 pounds]. He's athletic. He flies. He plays good defense and swings the bat well." *Mahoning Valley Scrappers*.

Below: The 2010 Scrappers alumni Shane Bieber, baseball's short 2020 season Cy Young winner. He achieved pitching's coveted Triple Crown along the way. He led the American League in wins, strikeouts and ERA. Bieber was seemingly on his way to repeat as the best pitcher on baseball after a monster start in 2021 but was shut down for several months with a sore shoulder. *Mahoning Valley Scrappers*.

Above: Happy Scrappers fans. *Mahoning Valley Scrappers.*

Left: Another snippet of history: Harry Stevens's program of the historic September 27, 1940 "Giebell game." Unknown Detroit Tigers pitcher Floyd Giebell beat Cleveland Indians ace and twenty-seven-game winner Bob Feller to win the pennant by one game for the Bengals. *Author's collection.*

to left to make the score 8–6. The beleaguered Shaw was replaced by Trevor Bauer, who put out the fire with no further damage.

In the Tribe tenth, Cubs reliever Carl Edwards Jr. got two quick outs before surrendering a walk to Brandon Guyer, who promptly advanced to second. That brought to the plate Rajai Davis, who promptly lined a daisy-cutter single to center field as Guyer crossed home, making it a one-run game. Mike Montgomery then replaced Cubs pitcher Edwards. Montgomery promptly retired the Indians' last hope, Michael Martinez, to win the world championship for the Chicago Cubs after a hiatus of 108 seasons.

The Indians/Guardians still wait.

BASEBALL REMAINS ALIVE AND well at Eastwood Field. According to Matt Thompson, the Scrappers' assistant general manager: "Following the developmental realignment by Major League Baseball, the Mahoning Valley Scrappers became one of the founding members of the MLB Draft League for the 2021 season. This new league has been set up as a proving ground for top level amateur prospects to highlight their skills before the draft. In simpler terms, this means that folks from the Mahoning Valley still have an affordable place to grab a hot dog and enjoy great baseball with family and friends."

THE MAHONING VALLEY SCRAPPERS

A SHORT HISTORY

*T*hese tables are an overview of the Mahoning Valley Scrappers seasons from 1999 through 2022. Their records, managers and final standings within the division are included. They also list players who later reached the majors and any Tribe or Guardians postseason/World Series appearance(s) (PS/WS).

TABLE 1. 1999 MAHONING VALLEY SCRAPPERS (43-33, 1ST MCNAMARA)—MANAGER TED KUBIAK

Name	Pos.	PS/WS	Other
Victor Martinez	C	2007	16-yr MLB: 8166 AB, 246 HR, .295 BA. LL OBP (.409) 2014/Tigers. 10 yrs./Tribe. Also w/Red Sox. Possible HOF?
C.C. Sabathia	P	2001/07	19-yr MLB: 251-161 W-L, 3.74 ERA., 3093 Ks. 104 W/Tribe. Six-time AS. Cy Young winner. Possible HOF?
Ryan Drese	P	2001	6-yr MLB: 2/Tribe.
Kyle Denney	P	NO	1-year career with Tribe
Carl Sadler	P	NO	2-year career, 1 with Tribe

Table 2. 2000 Mahoning Valley Scrappers (48-28, 1st Pinkney)—
Manager Ted Kubiak

Name	Pos.	PS/WS	Other
Ryan Church	CF	NO	9-year career, .264 lifetime BA
Joe Inglett	2B	NO	6-year career, 1 with Tribe
Eric Crozier	OF-1B	NO	1-yr MLB. 2004 Blue Jays.
Hector Luna	SS	NO	8-year career, 1 with Tribe
John McDonald	SS	2001	On rehab assignment
Brian Tallet	P	NO	10-year career, 3 with Tribe
Carl Sadler	P	NO	2nd year with Scrappers

Table 3. 2001 Mahoning Valley Scrappers (26-49, 7th Pinkney)—
Manager Dave Turgeon

Name	Pos.	PS/WS	Other
Jon Van Every	OF	NO	3-year career, Played for Boston Red Sox
Mike Edwards	3B	NO	4-year career
Zach Sorensen	SS	NO	2-year career, 1 with Tribe
Josh Bard	C	NO	11-year career, 4 with Tribe

Table 4. 2002 Mahoning Valley Scrappers (46-30, 2nd Pinkney)—
Manager Chris Bando

Name	Pos.	PS/WS	Other
Jon Van Every	OF	NO	2nd year with Scrappers
Ben Francisco	OF	2007	7-yr MLB: 1579 AB, .253 BA, 199 R, 50 HRs. Played with Tribe, Yanks, Rays, Astros, Phillies.
Eider Torrez	SS	NO	1 year with Baltimore

Name	Pos.	PS/WS	Other
Einer Diaz	C	2001	Rehab assignment. Played with Cleveland (1996–2002), 10-year career
Marshall McDougall	3B	NO	Played with Texas 1 year
Brian Slocum	P	NO	Played with Indians (2006–8)
Roberto Hernandez	P	2007	AKA Fausto Carmona. 11 yr MLB: 71-99 W-L, 4.60 ERA. 19-8 W-L w/2007 Tribe. Dominican Republic.

TABLE 5. 2003 MAHONING VALLEY SCRAPPERS (38-36, 2ND PINKNEY)—MANAGER TED KUBIAK

Name	Pos.	PS/WS	Other
Brad Snyder	OF	NO	Played for Chicago Cubs and Texas Rangers
Kevin Kouzmanoff	3B	NO	7-year career, played 16 games with Tribe
Ryan Garko	OF	2007	6-year career, 5 with Tribe
Chris Magruder	OF	NO	5-year career, 2 with Indians
Jon Van Every	OF	NO	3rd consecutive year with Scrappers
Juan Lara	P	2007	Serious injury curtailed promising career. Had minor role in 2007 Tribe season.
Chad Durbin	P	NO	14-year career. played 1 year with Cleveland
John McDonald	SS	2001	Second rehab assignment
Paul Ringdon	P	NO	2-year career, played with Indians and Milwaukee Brewers

TABLE 6. 2004 MAHONING VALLEY SCRAPPERS (42-32, 2ND PINKNEY)—
MANAGER MIKE SARBAUGH

Name	Pos.	PS/WS	Other
Argenis Reyes	C	NO	2-yr MLB: .205 BA. Born in the Dominican Republic. Played with the New York Mets.
Chris Gimenez	3B-OF	2016	Backup 2016. 10-yrs MLB: 927 AB, .218 BA. Played with Rays, Rangers, Twins, Cubs and Tribe.
Wyatt Toregas	C	NO	2-yr MLB: .164 BA, 51 AB. Played in Cleveland, Pittsburgh.
Lou Merloni	2B-3B	NO	9-yr MLB: 1085 AB, .271 BA, 125 RBIs. Played with Red Sox, Padres, Angels, Indians. "Sweet Lou" is a sportscaster.
Aaron Laffey	P	2007	8-yr MLB: 9 AB, .222 BA. Defensive guru for Tribe, Mets, Mariners, Rockies, Yankees.
Tony Sipp	P	NO	26-22 W-L, 3.72 ERA in 616 MLB Games.
Mike Porzio	P	NO	3-yr MLB: 3-3 W-L, 5.90 ERA. Played with 3 teams.
Scott Lewis	P	NO	2-yr MLB: 4-0 W-L, 3.49 ERA. Played with Tribe entire career.
Brian Tallet	P	NO	9-yr MLB: 16-25 W-L, 4.79 ERA

Table 7. 2005 Mahoning Valley Scrappers (33-43, 3rd Pinkney)—
Manager Rouglas Odor

Name	Pos.	PS/WS	Other
Jose Constanza	OF	NO	Dominican Republic. 4-yr MLB: .273 BA, 220 AB, 17 RBIs. Played for Atlanta Braves.
Jordan Brown	OF	NO	2-yr MLB
Trevor Crowe	OF	NO	4-yr MLB: 265 G, .240 BA. Played w/Cleveland, Houston.
Chad Zerbe	P	NO	4-yr MLB: 6-1 W-L, 3.87 ERA
Kevin Kouzmanoff	OF-3B	NO	2nd year with Scrappers
Kyle Denney	P	NO	1-yr MLB: 1-2 9.56 ERA. w/ Tribe
Scott Lewis	P	NO	2nd year with Scrappers
Jensen Lewis	P	2007	1-1 W-L, 2.15 ERA w/2007 Tribe
Matt Miller	P	NO	5-yr MLB: 6-1 W-L, 2.72 ERA. Entire career w/Cleveland.
Jason Stafford	P	2007	2-yr MLB: 2-5 W-L, 2.61 ERA

Table 8. 2006 Mahoning Valley Scrappers (36-34, 3rd Pinkney)—
Manager Rouglas Odor

Name	Pos.	PS/WS	Other
Matt McBride	C	NO	4-yr MLB: .201 BA. Played for Colorado Rockies, A's.
Josh Rodriguez	SS	NO	1-year career; 12 plate appearances.
Josh Tomlin	P	2016/17	13-9 W-L in 2016 and 10-9 W-L in 2017. Beat Cubs 1-0 on the road in 2016 World Series w/father in the stands.

Name	Pos.	PS/WS	Other
Neil Wagner	P	NO	3-yr MLB: 2-4 W-L, 4.92 ERA
JD Martin	P	NO	2-yr MLB: 6-9 W- L, 4.32 ERA
David Huff	P	NO	8-yr MLB: 25-30 W-L, 5.17 ERA

TABLE 9. 2007 MAHONING VALLEY SCRAPPERS (37-37, 2ND PINKNEY)—
MANAGER TIM LAKER

Name	Pos.	PS/WS	Other
Josh Judy	P	NO	No decisions in a 1-yr career. On the roster of the 2011 Cleveland Indians.
Vinnie Pestano	P	NO	6-yrs MLB: 6-8 W-L 2.98 ERA

TABLE 10. 2008 MAHONING VALLEY SCRAPPERS (31-44, 5TH PINKNEY)—
MANAGER TRAVIS FRYMAN

Name	Pos.	PS/WS	Other
Lonnie Chisenhall	SS	2016/17	Tribe 5 seasons. Active in 2022.
Cord Phelps	2B	NO	4-year career, 3 with Cleveland
Matt Langwell	P	NO	1-yr MLB: 1-0 W-L, 5.14 ERA
Zach Putnam	P	NO	7-yr MLB: 10-7 W-L, 3.20 ERA

TABLE 11. 2009 MAHONING VALLEY SCRAPPERS (49-27, 1ST PINKNEY)—
MANAGER TRAVIS FRYMAN

Name	Pos.	PS/WS	Other
Jason Kipnis	2B	2016/17	9 yrs./Tribe:123 HRs, 135 SB's. 4404 AB, .260 BA. Also Cubs
Roberto Perez	C	2016/17	8 yrs./Tribe: 55 HRs, 1505 AB, .233 BA

Name	Pos.	PS/WS	Other
Preston Gullmet	P	NO	5-yrs. MLB. Tribe, Orioles, Tampa, Toronto, Brewers, Miami
Austin Adams	P	NO	6-yrs. MLB: 6-4 W-L, 3.90 ERA
Tyler Sturdivant	P	NO	Played with Tampa Bay Devil Rays
Cory Burns	P	NO	2-yr MLB: 1-1 W-L. 2 teams
Vidal Nuno	P	NO	6-yr MLB: 8-21 W-L

TABLE 12. 2010 MAHONING VALLEY SCRAPPERS (36-34, 3RD PINKNEY)—MANAGER TRAVIS FRYMAN

Name	Pos.	PS/WS	Other
Carlos Moncrieff	C	NO	1 year with San Francisco Giants
Josh Rodriguez	SS	NO	1 season with Pittsburgh Pirates
Josh Tomlin	P	2016/17	2nd year with Scrappers
Neil Wagner	P	NO	3-yr MLB
David Huff	P	NO	8-year career
Josh Tomlin	P	YES	13–9 for 2016 pennant winners
Gio Urshela	3B	2017	7-yr MLB: 256 RBIs
Jesus Aguilar	1B	2016	9-yr MLB: 109 HRs
Wyatt Toregas	C	NO	2-yr MLB: 21 G
Mitch Talbot	P	NO	3-yr MLB: 12-19 W-L

TABLE 13. 2011 MAHONING VALLEY SCRAPPERS (36-34, 3RD PINKNEY)—MANAGER DAVID WALLACE

Name	Pos.	PS/WS	Other
Tony Wolters	C	NO	Still playing in 2022
Erik Gonzalez	SS	2016/17	Played with Scrappers in 2011 and 2012.

Name	Pos.	PS/WS	Other
Francisco Lindor	P	2016/17	2016 World Series hero, still playing in 2022 (NY Mets)
Joseph Colon	P	2016	Played with Cleveland in 2016
Cody Allen	P	2016/17	2016 World Series hero, 7 seasons with Tribe, 153 saves
Drew Rucinski	P	NO	4-year career
Elvis Araujo	P	NO	2 years with Philadelphia
Cody Anderson	P	2016	Pitched 19 games with 2016 pennant winners
Shawn Armstrong	P	2016/17	8-yr MLB: 7-5 W-L, 4.57 ERA
Jeanmar Gomez	P	NO	10-year career, born in Venezuela
Hector Rondon	P	NO	8-year career with Chicago
Jordan Smith	P	NO	2-yr MLB: 3-2 W-L, 4.94 ERA

TABLE 14. 2012 MAHONING VALLEY SCRAPPERS (30-45, 5TH PINKNEY)—MANAGER TED KUBIAK

Name	Pos.	PS/WS	Other
Erik Gonzalez	1B-3B	2016/17	6-year career, played 3 seasons with Tribe
Joey Wendle	2B-3B	NO	6-year career
Robel Garcia	2B-SS	NO	2-year career with Chicago and Houston
Hunter Jones	OF	NO	Played hockey, 2-year career with Boston and Florida
Tyler Naquin	CF	2016/17	2016 World Series hero, 6-year career, 5 with Cleveland
Eric Haase	C	NO	4-year career, 2 with Tribe
Jose Ramirez	2B-SS	2016/17/22	Clutch hitting, post season hero. 9-year career, all with Cleveland

Name	Pos.	PS/WS	Other
Ryan Merritt	P	2016	Played 2 seasons, both with Cleveland
Louis Head	P	NO	1-year career

TABLE 15. 2013 MAHONING VALLEY SCRAPPERS (30-44, 5TH PINKNEY)—MANAGER TED KUBIAK

Name	Pos.	PS/WS	Other
Robel Garcia	C	NO	2-yr MLB: .174 BA. Classic utilityman
Cole Sulser	SS	NO	4-yr MLB: 125 G, 7-13 W-L, 3.75 ERA. Tampa, Orioles, Miami
Ben Heller	P	NO	5-yr MLB: 2-0 W-L, 2.59 ERA 31 G. New York Yankees
Kyle Crockett	P	2016/17	4-yr MLB: 5-1 W-L, 3.74 ERA 73 K's. Tribe, A's, Reds, AZ
Brett Myers	P	NO	12-yr MLB: 97-96 W-L, 4.25 ERA. Tribe
Chris Perez	P	NO	7-year career, played with Cleveland 5 years
Blake Wood	P	NO	7-year career, played with Cleveland 2 years

TABLE 16. 2014 MAHONING VALLEY SCRAPPERS (33-42, 5TH PINKNEY)—MANAGER TED KUBIAK

Name	Pos.	PS/WS	Other
Francisco Mejin	C	2017	5-year career, 1 with Tribe, still playing in 2022
Greg Allen	C	2017	5-year career, 4 with Indians. .229 BA 2017.
Bradley Zimmer	RF-CF	2017	5-year career, still with Guardians in 2022

Name	Pos.	PS/WS	Other
Cam Hill	P	NO	2-0 W-L 4.19 ERA for 2020 Tribe
Julian Merryweather	P	NO	Played 2 years with Toronto
JP Feyereisen	P	NO	Still playing in 2022
TJ House	P	2016	Pitched 4 G 2016 Tribe, no decisions.
Nick Maronde	P	NO	3 seasons with Los Angeles Angels

TABLE 17. 2015 MAHONING VALLEY SCRAPPERS (31-44, 6TH PINKNEY)—
MANAGER TRAVIS FRYMAN

Name	Pos.	PS/WS	Other
Willi Castro	C	NO	3-year career, all with Detroit
Ka'ai Tom	SS	NO	1-year career, played with Oakland and Pittsburgh
Mark Mathias	P	NO	Played in 2020 with Milwaukee
Sam Haggerty	P	NO	Played 3 years
Anthony Santander	P	NO	Played 5 years with Baltimore
Sam Hentges	P	2022	3-2 W-L in 2022, 63 G, 2.45 ERA
Josh Tomlin	P	2016/17	2019 World Series hero, 9 seasons with Cleveland. 2022.
Nick Hagadone	P	NO	5-year career, all with Tribe

TABLE 18. 2016 MAHONING VALLEY SCRAPPERS (37-38, 4TH PINKNEY)—
MANAGER EDWIN RODRIGUEZ

Name	Pos.	PS/WS	Other
Shane Bieber	P	2022	13-8 W-L, 2.88 ERA 2022. W G 1 PO 2022. 2020 Cy Young.
Aaron Civale	P	2022	5-6 W-L, 4.92 ERA in 2022. Pitched 20 G.

Michael Brantley	OF	2016/17	Rehab assignment
Oscar Gonzalez	LF	2022	.296 BA, clutch playoff HR in 15th advanced 2022 Guardians.
Triston McKenzie	P	2022	11-11 W- L in 2022. 2.96 ERA 2022 Guardians, W PO G 2.
Tanner Tully	P	2022	3 G, 6 IP, 6.00 ERA, 0-0 W-L in 2022

TABLE 19. 2017 MAHONING VALLEY SCRAPPERS (44-29, 1ST PINKNEY)—MANAGER LUKE CARLIN

Name	Pos.	PS/WS	Other
Ernie Clement	2B	2022	Batted .200 in limited role w/2022 Guardians.
Francisco Perez	P	NO	1-year career, played with Cleveland in 2021
Elijah Morgan	P	2022	5-3 W-L 3.38 ERA, 2022 Cleveland Guardians
Kyle Nelson	P	NO	Played 2 years with Cleveland
Zach Plesac	P	2022	3-12 W-L, 4.31 ERA, 2022 Guardians
James Karinchack	P	2022	2-0 W-L, 2.08 ERA with 3 saves on 2022 Guardians.
Sam Hentges	P	2022	Second year with Scrappers. On 2022 Guardians playoff team.
Josh Tomlin	P	2016/17	Rehab assignment
Danny Salazar	P	2016	2016 World Series hero
Jean Carlos Mejia	P	NO	Played with Cleveland in 2021
Will Benson	RF	2022	.250 OBP in limited role w/ 2022 Guardians.
Oscar Gonzalez	LF	2022	.296 BA w/2022 Guardians. HR in 15th W 2022 PS G 2.

Name	Pos.	PS/WS	Other
Nolan Jones	3B	2022	.244 BA w/2022 Guardians
Kirk McCarty	P	2022	2022 rookie, 4-3 W-L, 4.54 ERA

Table 20. 2018 Mahoning Valley Scrappers (42-33, 1st Pinkney)—Manager Jim Pankovits

Name	Pos.	PS/WS	Other
Cody Anderson	P	2016	2-5 W-L 4.84 ERA 2016. 3 yr MLB, all with Cleveland.
Luis Oviedo	P	NO	1-2 W-L w/2021 Cleveland Indians.
Justin Garza	P	NO	2021, only year in MLB
Tyler Freeman	2B, SS	2022	Batted .247 as backup utility player on 2022 Guardians.
Steven Kwan	OF	2022	ROY candidate for 2022 Guardians: .298 BA, scored 89 runs.
Richie Palacios	2B, SS	2022	.232 BA for 2022 Guardians.

Table 21. 2019 Mahoning Valley Scrappers (37-39, 4th Pinkney)—Manager Jim Pankovits

Name	Pos.	PS/WS	Other
Danny Otero	P	2016/17	Rehab assignment, 30 G for 2016 pennant winner, 5-1 record
Cam Hill	P	NO	2nd year with Scrappers
Francisco Perez	P	NO	Dominican Republic native. No decisions in 2 MLB seasons.
Wil Brennan	2B, SS	2022	Batted .364 in his first week as a late-season callup 2022.
Cam Hill	P	NO	2nd season with the Scrappers.
Bryan Lavastida	C	2022	Backup catcher on 2022 playoff squad.

| Hunter Gaddis | P | 2022 | 0-2 W-L on 2022 Guardians in 2 games. |
| Yanier Diaz | 3B | 2017 | Rehab assignment |

TABLE 22. 2020 MAHONING VALLEY SCRAPPERS (0-0)
Season canceled due to COVID-19

TABLE 23. 2021 MAHONING VALLEY SCRAPPERS (27-28, 2 3RD MLB
DRAFT LEAGUE)—MANAGER COCO CRISP

Name	Pos.	PS/WS	Other
Coco Crisp	X	2016	30 G 2016

TABLE 24. 2022 MAHONING VALLEY SCRAPPERS. (32-47) 6TH MLB
DRAFT LEAGUE. MANAGER—HOMER BUSH

Abbreviations: G= Games, AB= At Bats, K's= Strike outs, SO= Strikeouts,
W-L= Won-Loss Record, AS= All Star, OBP= On Base Percentage

All-Star Scrappers 2009 alumni Jason Kipnis, 2016 Believeland Indians star. The second baseman played a major role in the pennant run of 2016. Batting in the number-two position, Kipnis displayed much power, hitting twenty-three home runs, with ninety-one runs scored, 168 hits, eighty-three RBIs and a slugging percentage of .469. Kipnis homered, doubled and singled in the same game of multiple Fall Classic contests (Games 4 and 6). *Mahoning Valley Scrappers.*

All-Star 2012 Scrappers alumni Jose Ramirez, a 2016 Believeland Indians star. The switch-hitting third baseman reached the MLB in 2013. "No Way Jose" has played his entire career with Cleveland. Ramirez came into his own during the Tribe's pennant-winning season of 2016. The popular infielder is the subject of many commercial items, including salsa products and T-shirts, including one that reads, "When the boogeyman goes to sleep, he checks the closet for Jose Ramirez." *Mahoning Valley Scrappers*.

The 2011 Scrappers alumni Cody Anderson. Though largely ignored as a rookie in 2015, Anderson set a team record for the fewest runs allowed in his first four starts (with three). *Mahoning Valley Scrappers*.

Right-handed All-Star 2009 Scrappers alumni Cody Allen was a 2016 Believeland Indians hero and has been named the Indians/Guardians all-time best reliever, with 149 career saves. Allen made his MLB debut in 2012. In 2016, he appeared in sixty-seven games, recorded thirty-two regular season saves, struck out eighty-seven in sixty-eight innings pitched, posted a 2.51 ERA and an even 1.00 WHIP. In the postseason, Allen overpowered the opposition, appearing in ten of Cleveland's fifteen postseason games. He did not allow a run, logged six saves and struck out twenty-four. *Mahoning Valley Scrappers.*

The 2006 Scrappers alumni Josh Tomlin, a true 2016 Believeland Indians star. He advanced to the big leagues in 2013 and came into his own during the Tribe's 2016 pennant-winning campaign, winning his first seven decisions. *Mahoning Valley Scrappers*.

BIBLIOGRAPHY

The Prelude

Achorn, Edward. *Fifty-Nine in '84: Old Hoss Radbourn, Barehanded Baseball, and the Greatest Season a Pitcher Ever Had*. Washington, DC: Smithsonian, 2010.

Cleveland Leader, August 11, 1883.

Felber, Bill. *Inventing Baseball: The 100 Greatest Games of the 19th Century*. Phoenix, AZ: Society for American Baseball Research SABR, 2013.

Laing, Jeffery Michael. *Bud Fowler: Baseball's First Black Professional*. Jefferson, NC: McFarland & Company, 2019.

Lancaster (PA) Intelligencer, September 1883.

Niles (OH) Daily Times. "E Wilson Recalls Interesting Days When Niles' Professional Baseball Team Played Cleveland Nine Here / Bud Fowler… Made the Baseball Do Tricks." Centennial edition, 1934.

Plain Dealer (Cleveland, OH), August 11, 1883.

Winchester, Simon. *Krakatoa: The Day the World Exploded*. New York: HarperCollins, 2003.

Chapter 1

Laing, Jeffrey Michael. *Bud Fowler: Baseball's First Black Professional*. Jefferson, NC: McFarland & Company, 2013.

Niles Daily Times. "E Wilson Recalls Interesting Days When Niles' Professional Baseball Team Played Cleveland Nine Here / Bud Fowler….Made the Ball Do Tricks." Centennial edition, 1934.

Chapter 2

Achorn, Edward. *Fifty-Nine in '84: Old Hoss Radbourn, Barehanded Baseball, and the Greatest Season a Pitcher Ever Had*. Washington, DC: Smithsonian, 2010.

Cleveland Daily Leader, August 11, 1883.

Daily City News (New Castle, PA), April 16, 1883.

Drake, Thomas D. "Del Drake." *National Pastime: A Review of Baseball History* 21 (2001).

Felber, Bill. *Inventing Baseball: The 100 Greatest Games of the 19th Century*. Phoenix, AZ: Society for American Baseball Research, 2013.

Laing, Jeffrey Michael. *Bud Fowler: Baseball's First Black Professional*. Jefferson, NC: McFarland & Company, 2013.

Lancaster Intelligencer, 1883.

Niles Daily Times. "E Wilson Recalls Interesting Days When Niles' Professional Baseball Team Played Cleveland Nine Here / Bud Fowler…Made the Ball Do Tricks." Centennial edition, 1934.

Plain Dealer, August 11, 1883.

Weekly Jeffersonian (Findlay, OH), July 20, 1899.

Chapter 3

Cleveland Daily Leader. "A Cold-Blooded Murder." July 29, 1864.

History of Niles, Ohio. Niles, OH: Niles Centennial History Club, 2008.

Niles Daily Times. "E Wilson Recalls Interesting Days When Niles' Professional Baseball Team Played Cleveland Nine Here / Bud Fowler….Made the Ball Do Tricks." Centennial edition, 1934.

Western Reserve Chronicle (Warren, OH). "Home Intelligence." March 26, 1856.

———. "Niles." August 15, 1883.

———. "Trial of Francis O. Robbins for the Murder of James Ward." December 7, 1864.

Chapter 4

Denney, Robert E. *The Civil War Years: A Day-to-Day Chronicle*. New York: Gramercy Books, 1992.

Foote, Shelby. *The Civil War: A Narrative*. Vol. 3, *Red River to Appomattox*. New York: Knopf, Vintage Civil War Library, 1986.

Frederickson, John C. *Civil War Almanac*. New York: Checkmark Books, 2007.

Chapter 5

Egan, James M. Jr. *Baseball on the Western Reserve: The Early Game in Cleveland and Northeast Ohio, Year by Year and Town by Town, 1865–1900*. Jefferson, NC: McFarland & Company, 2008.

Nemec, David. *The Rank and File of 19th Century Major League Baseball: Biographies of 1,084 Players, Owners, Managers and Umpires*. Jefferson, NC: McFarland & Company, 2012.

Chapter 6

Egan, James M. Jr. *Baseball on the Western Reserve: The Early Game in Cleveland and Northeast Ohio, Year by Year and Town by Town, 1865–1900*. Jefferson, NC: McFarland & Company, 2008.

Fort Wayne (IN) News, July 22, 1899

Laing, Jeffrey Michael. *Bud Fowler; Baseball's First Black Professional*. Jefferson, NC: McFarland & Company, 2013.

Lutzke, Mitch. *The Page Fence Giants; A History of Black Baseball's Pioneering Champions*. Jefferson, NC: McFarland & Company, 2018.

Nemec, David. *The Rank and File of 19th Century Major League Baseball: Biographies of 1,084 Players, Owners, Managers, and Umpires*. Jefferson, NC: McFarland & Company, 2012

Newton (KS) Daily Republican, April 3, 1890.

Omaha (NE) Daily Bee, February 1, 1891.

Pittsburgh Post-Gazette, September 13, 1899.

Riley, James A. *Biographical Encyclopedia of the Negro Baseball Leagues*. New York: Carroll & Graf, 1994.

Sterling (KS) Post-Gazette, September 13, 1890.

Watertown (MA) News, May 27, 1891; June 24, 1891; July 1, 1891; July 22, 1891.

Chapter 7

Encyclopedia Britannica. "Spanish-American War."
Niles Daily Times, December 20, 1927; January 29, 1943.
Washington Post, April 23, 1897.
Weekly Leavenworth (KS) Post, March 26, 1897.
Wikipedia. "Theodore Roosevelt." www.en.wikipedia.org.
Will-Weber, Mark. *Muskets and Applejack: Spirits, Soldiers, and the Civil War.* Washington, DC: Regnery History, 2017.

Chapter 8

Buffalo (NY) Enquirer, August 18, 1898; August 16, 1899.
Brooklyn (NY) Daily Eagle, n.d.
Hickman (NE) Enterprises, May 5, 1897.
Inter Ocean (Chicago), October 15, 1897.
Niles Daily Times, July 9, 1910; June 16, 1914; March 13, 1923; November 30, 1931.
Sioux City (IA) Journal, December 2, 1936.
Youngstown (OH) Vindicator, November 30, 1931.
Wilkes-Barre (PA) Record, February 28, 1912.

Chapter 9

Cleveland Press, October 3, 1895.
Egan, James M. Jr. *Baseball on the Western Reserve: The Early Game in Cleveland and Northeast Ohio, Year by Year and Town by Town.* Jefferson, NC: McFarland and Company, 1953.
Fleitz, David L. *Rowdy Patsy Tebeau and the Cleveland Spiders: Fighting to the Bottom of Baseball, 1887–1899.* Jefferson, NC: McFarland & Company, 2017.
Krsolovic, Ken, and Bryan Fritz. *League Park: Historic Home of Cleveland Baseball.* Jefferson, NC: McFarland and Company, 1958.
Lee, Bill. *The Baseball Necrology: The Post Baseball Lives and. Deaths of over 7,600 Major League Players and Others.* Jefferson, NC: McFarland & Company, 2003.
Nemec, David, *The Rank and File of 19ᵗʰ Century Major League Baseball: Biographies of 1,084 Players, Owners, Managers, and Umpires.* Jefferson, NC: McFarland & Company, 2012.

Phillips, John. *Buck Ewing and the 1893 Cleveland Spiders*. Brooksville, FL: Capital Publishing Company 1992.

———. *The 1895 Cleveland Spiders Temple Cup Champions*. Brooksville, FL: Capital Publishing Company 1990.

———. *The Fall Classics of the 1890s*. Brooksville, FL: Capital Publishing Company 1989.

———. *Uncle Nick's Birthday Party*. N.p.: self-published, 1991

Schlossberg, Dan. *The New Baseball Bible: Notes, Nuggets, Lists, and Legends from Our National Pastime*. New York: Sports Publishing, 2002, 2017.

Chapter 10

Belson, Ted. *New York Times*. "23-Year-Old Eats His Way to Hot Dog Title." July 4, 2007 .

Durso, Joseph. "Score-Card Harry's Family." In *Harry M. Stevens Yearbook: Celebrating Our 100th Anniversary*. Souvenir Edition. New York: Harry M. Stevens, n.d.

Nagler, Barney, "Harry's Scorecard." In *Harry M. Stevens Yearbook: Celebrating Our 100th Anniversary*. Souvenir Edition. New York: Harry M. Stevens, n.d.

A Pictorial History of Niles, Ohio. Bicentennial Edition. Niles Historical Society, Niles, Ohio, 1976.

Stevens, Harry M. "An Ounce of Invention." In *Harry M. Stevens Yearbook: Celebrating Our 100th Anniversary*. Souvenir Edition. New York: Harry M. Stevens, n.d.

Chapter 11

Town Talk [Alexandria, LA], June 13, 1963.

Chapter 12

Feller, Bob. *Bob Feller's Strikeout Story*. New York: Grosset & Dunlap, 1947.

———. *Pitching to Win*. New York: Grosset & Dunlap, 1948, 1952.

Gilbert, Bill. *Now Pitching, Bob Feller*. Secaucus, NJ: Carol Publishing Group, 1990.

School, Gene. *Bob Feller: Hall of Fame Strikeout Star*. New York: Doubleday & Company, 1962.

Sher, Jack. "Bob Feller and His Dad." *Reader's Digest*, July 1947.
Sickles, John. *Bob Feller: Ace of the Greatest Generation*. Brassey's Inc., 2004.

Chapter 13

Jones, David. *Baseball Stars of the American League*. Sterling, VA: Potomac Books Inc., 2006.
Kovach, Paul. "Remembrance of the Men of Old." *The Dirt*, July 2007.
Nemec, David. *SABR Major League Baseball Profiles: 1871–1900*. Vol. 2, *The Hall of Famers and Memorable Personalities Who Shaped the Game*. Lincoln: University of Nebraska Press, 2011.
Phillips, John. *Bill Hinchman's Boner and the 1908 Cleveland Naps*. Brooksville, FL: Capital Publishing Company, 1990.
———. *When Lajoie Came to Town: The Story of the Cleveland Blues of 1902*. Brooksville, FL: Capital Publishing Company, 1988.

Chapter 14

Niles Daily News, October 13, 1920.
Phillips, John. *The 1920 Indians*. Brooksville, FL: Capital Publishing, 1989.
Schneider, Russell. *The Cleveland Indians Encyclopedia*. Philadelphia, PA: Temple University Press, 1996.

Chapter 15

Prebenna, David. *The Complete Baseball Encyclopedia: The Complete and Official Record of Major League Baseball*. New York: MacMillan, 1990.
Riley, James A. *The Biographical Encyclopedia of the Negro Baseball Leagues*. New York: Carroll & Graff Publishers, 1994.
Swank, Michael T., Ted Toles Jr., Danielle Brassard and Ted Toles III. *Living on Borrowed Time: The Life and Times of Negro League Player Ted Toles Jr.* N.p.: MichaelTSwank, 2014.

Chapter 16

Brown, John. Interview with author. December 7, 2021.
Mahoning Valley Scrappers 1998 Yearbook.

Chapter 17

Mahoning Valley Scrappers Archives.

Chapter 18

Akron (OH) Beacon Journal, June 26, 2016; September 17, 2016.
Chicago Tribune, September 26, 2016.
Daily Journal (Flat River, MO), October 5, 2016.
Daily Sentinel (Grand Junction, CO) October 1, 2016.
Los Angeles Times, October 2, 2016.

ABOUT THE AUTHOR

P.M. KOVACH is a lifelong baseball fan. This is his first book on the subject.

Visit us at
www.historypress.com
....